Romance & the Cinema

General Editor
SHERIDAN MORLEY

Romance & the Cinema

JOHN KOBAL

Studio Vista · London

Published in Great Britain by Studio Vista Publishers
35 Red Lion Square London WC1

Made by Roxby Press Productions
55 Conduit Street London W1R 0NY
General Editor Sheridan Morley
Assistant Editor Bettina Tayleur
Picture Research John Kobal
Design & art direction Dodd and Dodd
Printed in Great Britain by Morrison & Gibb Limited
London and Edinburgh

ISBN 0 289 70423 5

FOREWORD

From Lillian Gish in *Broken Blossoms* through more than half a century to Ali McGraw in *Love Story*, romance has been as much a part of the cinema's history as celluloid itself; from Valentino and Harlow through to Paul Newman and Anouk Aimée, the great stars have as often been judged by their romantic appeal as by their acting ability, and with the possible exceptions of Lassie and Lon Chaney it is hard to think of many Hollywood stars, at least in the years before we made *From Here to Eternity*, who survived by being unromantic.

True, times have since changed, and in the 1950s and 60s the old flowers-and-frills were replaced by a more realistic, sometimes more brutal, approach to love. But as this book suggests, the cinema did never, perhaps will never, move far away from the romanticism of its early years and in the end maybe that is not a bad thing – we are all surely still entitled to our dreams even if they are now in Cinerama.

CHAPTER ONE

ROMANCE

What is it?

Who has it?

No-one can define 'romance' but we all think we know what it is. Romance is unfulfilled love; it is love not fully recognized; it is understatement. Romance is a song like 'One for My Baby and One More for the Road'; it is chiffon and ostrich feathers blown by the wind machines; it is the wind in the fur collar of Dietrich's coat after Clive Brook has left her; it is *Shanghai Express*; it is swirling skirts and waltzes; it is Garbo as *Camille* winning back the passionate young Armand, holding his tearful face in her hands and knowing that she has embarked on a fatal relationship. Marilyn Monroe was one of our generation's last great romantic figures. In *Bus Stop* she dreamed of success and happiness in terms of a mink coat. Near the end of the film, when she is about to begin life with the gauche, but adoring cowboy, she shivers as she steps into the cold and he places his battered wind-breaker around her shoulders. The moment Monroe brushes her cheek against the rabbit-collar you realize she has found her mink. That is romance.

Garbo in *Wild Orchids* **(1929).**

The movie screen is the face of love. The close-up and the dolly-shot are its means of communicating to us the most minute gesture and the subtlest of emotions, and so projecting the erotic power of the screen into the mind of the audience. In *A Place in The Sun* the close-up of the two young people dancing reveals the intensity of the passion between them; in *Madame Bovary* the sensuous and lyrical dolly-shot that Minnelli uses for the waltz sweeps us along in Emma's night of triumphant happiness; both shots convey the movements and the secrets of lovers and enable us to be at once both voyeur and lover.

From Mallarmé's poetry to the arts of déshabillé no nation has known better how to tap the founts of the bourgeoisie's erotic and romantic fantasies than the French. All the recorded arts of enticement, the subtleties of seduction and the studied ardour that is accepted for love, though not invented by the French, were certainly perfected and to the rest of us are symbolized by the French people. Such anyway is the boast of Paris. It is the recurrent theme of French writers from Laclos to Colette to Françoise Sagan. This image is one of the major sources of revenue for its tourist industry. The French have made a thriving industry out of everything to do with love – from food to perfume – falling short, and this, of course, is only one opinion, at love itself. Their stars simulate sexuality probably better than those of any other nation. Speaking any language other than their own, the French accent is the most seductive. Let me add here that Maurice Chevalier, that perennial embodiment of the romantic male, drove me up the wall. Whether speaking or singing he turned every 'Mimi', 'Mitzi' and 'Louise' into a trivial coquette. Charles Boyer's liquorice-stick accent was saved from the comical by his ability as an actor, but sometimes it skirted perilously close to parody in films that cast him as a romantic hero, as in *Algiers*. It doesn't matter that he never asked Hedy Lamarr to 'come wiz me to ze casbah'. It wasn't what he said but the way he said it that made audiences remember him for the one line he never spoke instead of for any he did. The same is true of their female exports. In English they become precious and self-conscious. The reason for this I think is that

FACES OF ROMANCE

Garbo and the beautiful young Robert Taylor in ***Camille.***

Cary Grant and Eve Marie Saint in ***North By Northwest.***

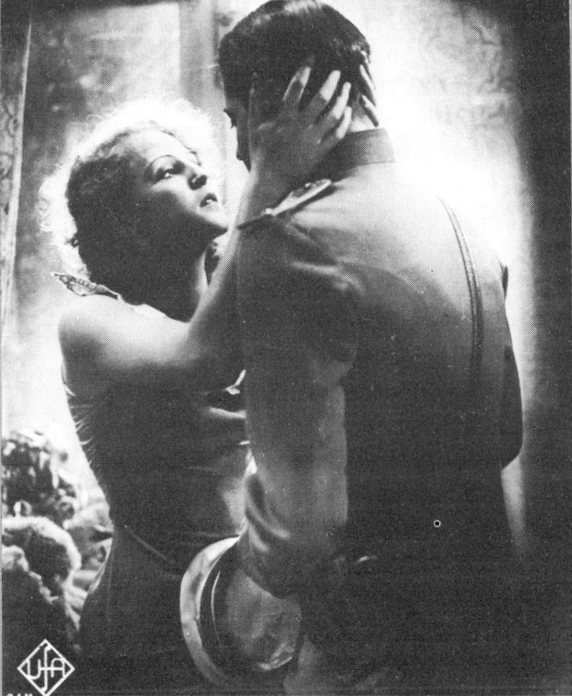

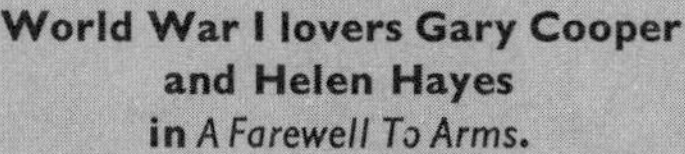

World War I lovers Gary Cooper and Helen Hayes in ***A Farewell To Arms.***

Birgitte Helm in *Die Wunderbare Luge Der Nina Petrovna* **with Francis Lederer.**

The hand belongs to Tyrone Power, the 'look' to Hildegarde Knef in ***Diplomatic Courier.***

we are more aware of the lack of warmth and the amount of artificiality that may charm the ear but mock the heart. One senses the simulation of a passion that could be turned on and off at the mention of price.

But there are stars for whom their nationality is the source and not the limit of their genius. Among these I would class Arletty, the early Jean Gabin and the later Danielle Darrieux, beginning with the films she made with Max Ophuls. She is never more French and at the same time more universal than when embodying to perfection Ophuls's butterfly heroines – the disillusioned wife in *La Ronde*; the trivial but finally pathetic *Madame De...*, and as the calculating inmate of *La Maison de Madame Tellier* – by far the best of the charming short stories that make up *Le Plaisir*, an exquisitely constructed tournament d'amour. In such films one gets an image that is the distillation of the French romantic cinema at its best. In profile and silk slip, late at night and alone in her room, Mlle. Darrieux stands by the open window overlooking the verdant countryside. From the cigarette erotically suspended in her hand, the curling smoke rises and mingles with the exhalation from her slightly parted lips. Her eyes open, looking out but seeing in. She is thinking about life in the country, lost innocence and the fact that Jean Gabin cannot sleep either. It is a scene of perfect harmony between director and star. This breathing stillness is, for me, one of the miracles of the cinema.

Romance in a glance between Clift and Taylor in ***A Place In The Sun*** **(1951).**

Apart from these exceptions and a few others, it has always struck me as perfectly in keeping with their general approach to romance that dirty photos the world over should be known as 'French postcards'; it is a natural extension of their supremacy in fashion (the artificial disguise of the human body) and in perfumes for women and in after-shaves for men. It is, judging from their romantic films, a fake romanticism, a lyricism of the camera but not the soul, a surface attraction incapable of giving birth to a timeless passion.

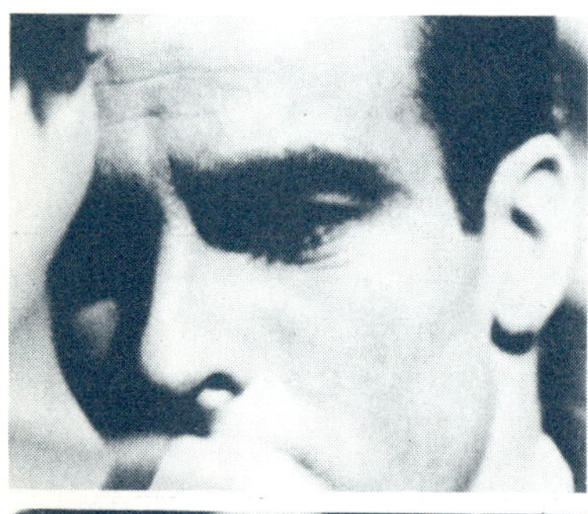

French Romantic Cinema as the world saw it could be said to have been exemplified in the work of Sacha Guitry. An urbane man, he was equally at home in the theatre as in the cinema, to which he turned fairly late in life in the mid-30s. He proceeded to make a popular series of films, most of which he wrote, directed and starred in. Guitry portrayed the manners and morals of his countrymen, most of which related to love, with great charm, good-humoured irony and with a wisdom that disarmed even his sternest critics. His films like *Faisons un Rêve* and *Roman d'un Tricheur* were as popular as they were penetrating, charged with an awareness of the mortality of all things especially love.

That other widely accepted purveyor of sentimental romanticism, the Austrian and German cinema, proves to me as synthetically fabricated on close examination. The charm of their best-known stars in their manner of speech, their emotion in a romantic setting, overlie a chasm of whipped-cream sentiments from which, once fallen in, recovery is rare. Initially few human sounds are quite as devastating and enchanting as Germanic attempts at English – relying more on the sounds the words can make in their butterscotch mouths than on their meaning – by the Austro/German/Hungarian actresses who have at one time or another gazed from the silver screens with childish innocence and trembling lips: Elizabeth Bergner, idol of the 30s; Louise Rainer, whose tearful 'Flow, Flow' on the telephone into Flo Ziegfeld's (William Powell) sugar-coated earlobes in the musical biography of his life, *The Great Ziegfeld*, is generally considered to have won her her first Oscar; the now forgotten Paula Wessely, whose starring debut in Willi Forst's superb *Maskerade* devastated public and critics across Europe, even though by the conventions of the glamour-conscious 30s she was decidedly stout and only modestly pretty; more recently the lachrymose appeal of Maria Schell – these and their Nordic sisters (Ingrid Bergman could be added though she has other strings to her long bow) created an initial impact outside their own milieu, going on to achieve a spectacular popularity almost unrivalled by any other foreign stars, only to fall faster and harder (often in a short space of time) in the public's affection and nearly always in critical esteem. There seems to have been a sneaking suspicion that the mysterious pull of such stars was not the siren's snare but the mother's apron strings, that not paradise but an oppressively cloying bedroom awaited those that succumbed to their charms; that anything so sugar-coated had to be a bitter pill underneath.

Passion on a poster (1930).

Looking around at other European countries, one finds something similar. The Italian cinema's public have always evinced a preference for high-flown operatic passion in keeping with their own lyrical, explosive temperament, which tourists adore but which exports, as far as their romantic favourites are concerned, too comically for them to achieve a similar popularity in less sun-drenched climates. Their exceptions prove the rule. Valentino went to America as a young man and in his short but sensational career in the 20s he enslaved an era and has ever since been the masculine personification of romantic love. No other Italian actor has even approached this international acclaim, not even Marcello Mastroianni of recent years whose popularity outside Italy has been more with the critics than with the public and whose successful films could hardly be said to have depended on him for their success. The same can be said of most of their romantic divas, few of whom have excited the same frenzied adulation as their progenitors in the golden age of the Italian cinema, between 1908 and 1920, Francesca Bertini or Lyda Borelli. Their popularity reached such astronomical heights that in the end it could be said that their lavish salaries caused the collapse of the Italian film industry. In the following years until the end of World War II only two names of international repute come to mind, Alida Valli and Isa Miranda, and only the Nordic beauty of Miss Miranda achieved true popularity wherever she worked. Post-war Italian stars have met with sporadic success abroad, though rarely in keeping with their frenzied popularity at home, much of it due to the 50s upsurge of interest in the mammary glands. Of these Gina Lollobrigida and Sophia Loren are the most famous examples, and Silvana Mangano a fascinating complex exception.

Love and Lubitsch spelled fun and games. Maurice Chevalier and Jeanette Macdonald in *One Hour With You* **(1932).**

With fewer Russian films to judge from, those seen suggest that their romanticism, with its source in their love of the land, could have a larger international appeal if it was not handicapped by having

CHARLES BOYER

French men, especially in American films, have always represented the apogee of romantic agony. Charles Boyer's smouldering features were well deployed in creating romantic havoc among Hollywood's top glamour girls. Audiences were fascinated by the fatalistic quality Boyer brought to most of his American films.

Marilyn Monroe rehearsing with real mink the joy she will feel with a rabbit-fur collar in *Bus Stop* (1956).

to pursue a politically acceptable outcome as well. For an epic life-style surges through their films – love is seen to be constructive and genuinely moving in its simplicity, in its sacrifice and in its warmth that strikes a universal chord, i.e. *Ballad of a Soldier* and *The Cranes are Flying*. If it was not for the intrusion of politically motivated situations as contrived as any Hollywood twist for the resolution of a happy end, I feel they would probably reach a wider audience. A case in point of a film that suffers from this externally enforced conflict can be seen in Grigori Chukrai's *The 41st*. In this story, set in the time of the Revolution, the militant Bolshevik heroine finds herself shipwrecked on an island with the White Russian officer she must kill. Alone on the island, dependent on each other, they fall in love. When rescue comes and they have a chance to escape together she recalls her greater love, i.e. her duty to socialist Russia, and shoots him. He is her 41st victim, though the first man she was involved with on a personal level, and her decision at the end is meant to be uplifting. One cannot avoid feeling, however, that this ending, besides being anti-romantic, is also unrealistic. The lesson one takes from such a solution is that countries and politics destroy where love has been shown to create. Obviously a worthier and more satisfying end would have been for them to start life together elsewhere. But in a Russian film that would have been tantamount to an attack on the system.

Unique among her fellow actresses was Arletty. A dark, ageless beauty belonging equally to the past as the present, she was LOVE in essence and simplicity, whether the mistress of a count or of a cheap crook.

It is its cultural heritage, its national sentiments and financial interests that give each country its character. The protective isolationist barriers (built up over centuries) which each country has to maintain its own and keep out foreign influence, combined with the particular effects of climate, landscape, religion, economy and language, invariably slow down exchange. Cultural boundaries, being the strongest expression of a people's identity, remain inviolate even when a country's physical boundaries have been changed. For every film made by country A that goes on to become successful in countries B, C and D, hundreds fail because their interest for foreign cultures is limited. Scandinavian audiences may be fascinated initially by films from Latin countries, but the basis of true and lasting understanding between them must depend on universal and instinctive responses, strong enough for a long-term bridging of interests.

A rare exception to the isolationist film public of most countries are the British, who, surrounded on all sides by water, but centrally heated by the gulf stream along its Southwestern coastline, have built up fewer mental barriers to foreign ideas and cultures, perhaps because of their historic dependence on the ocean to protect their interests. They have equally appreciated the sunny Italians and the cold Scandinavians. Though the British can appear detached, overall they have remained more open to outside influences – comforted as they are by the thought that the world's largest moat, the English channel, keeps them inviolate and gives them the time for assessment that other nations, not so secure, feel they cannot afford. Despite this, British films have been blander and of less interest than those made by more chauvinist nations. Their tolerance, on their terms and not necessarily on their territory, has evolved into a smugness that was evident from the films they made rather than those they went to see.

The inbred feeling of superiority and understatement have made their films heavy, while 'good breeding', whether real or simulated, has undermined their potential romantic stars. Their male stars have done service as complacent lovers or moustache-twirling sex-fiends. Their actresses have been Hollywood's favourites for roles demanding 'cool blonde lady-like types' and these have been enormously popular stars, but they have been type-cast more to symbolize a romantic past than to take part in a recognizable modern reality. As Madonnas, queens and officers' wives – facing nobly the Zulu, the Indian or the dastardly knave – they are much admired, but there has not been one English actress yet who could raise a sluggish film to those heights a Joan Crawford scales as a matter of course. The problem, until a few years ago, with British films was that they were pompously and trivially based on the theory that 'If it's English it's good'.

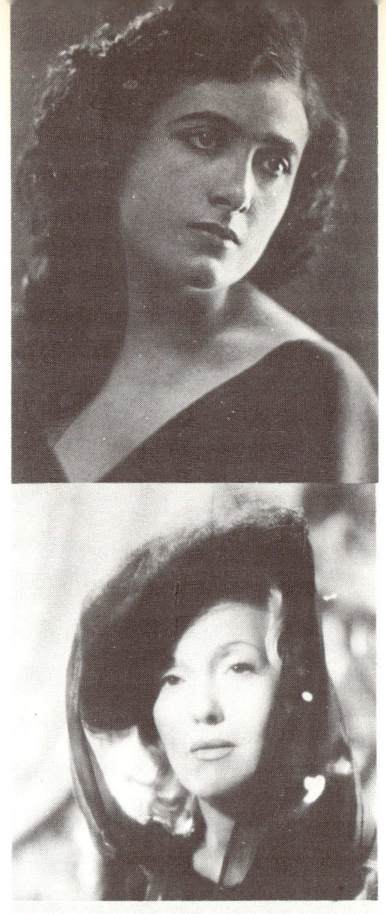

It has taken the American cinema to succeed where the others fail in creating the most internationally affecting romantic films and stars. They have managed to blend the most universally appealing signs of romance with the most universally acceptable situations into the most satisfying films. Of course, they were the ideal nation to do this and their success is not surprising. Drawing from material on every available source to feed the dreams of the most cosmopolitan assembly of people in one nation, they begin by removing all identifying traces of the source from the original – whether novel, opera, ballet, even folklore – putting it into a new form which would hold something that everyone could recognize and feel familiar with. The result stirs vague memories in most, while being dominated by none. The American romance has a universal appeal. Hollywood, in its market-researched, scientifically analysed audience-surveys, has learnt to create and to impose its non-denominational, but highly emotional, creation on to a sectarian world with amazing success. Even the name – Hollywood – which is a widespread suburb of the city of Los Angeles, has become synonymous the world over with romance: the romance of glamour, the romance of stardom. Those goals at the end of the rainbow that promise love.

What is accepted as an American film may be based on an English novel, may co-star a Frenchman and a Belgian leading lady, be set in Czarist Russia, with a screen-play worked on at various times by a German novelist, an Irish poetess and a Brooklyn gag-writer. The film will be produced by a Polish Jew who began his training for his future position in the rag-trade and ended up as arbiter of taste in the most influential medium of communication for the masses because he runs a film studio. Then, by an amazing alchemy, what comes out of this concoction will be an American film. The American is the most truly cosmopolitan man on earth. Not surprisingly then the films he produces are enjoyed wherever films are shown. By comparison, a French or German or Italian film on a similar subject to one made in Hollywood, will come out as an ethnically French or German or Italian film and its appeal will be limited because of it. Compare for example Hollywood's *Mata Hari* starring Greta Garbo and the French treatment of the same subject starring Jeanne Moreau. For every exception one could raise to my theory by citing an international

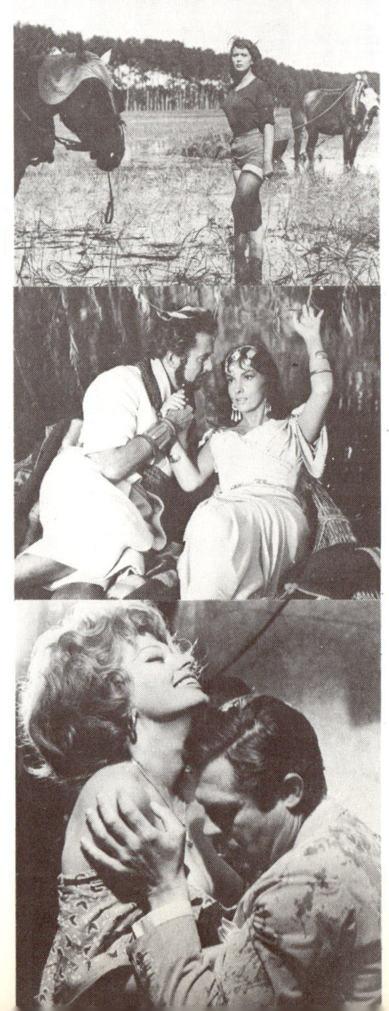

success like *Mayerling*, it must be apparent that there are hundreds more, equally fine, like *De Mayerling à Sarajavo*, that fail on the international market. The Americans specialize in following up a success with a string just like it and just as popular, if not always as good. In its time, the excellent Duvivier film *Pepe le Moko* may have stirred sophisticated art-house audiences, but it was the American re-make, *Algiers*, that became internationally successful a short time later, making Hedy Lamarr a sensation in her American debut, and consolidating Charles Boyer's popularity in the role of the great lover. Duvivier's film may have been more realistic and less glossy, but the American director John Cromwell and cameraman James Wong Howe created an infinitely more romantic movie. It is true, of course, that the Americans have invested more money in films as a paying proposition, but this would not have happened if they did not pay off, and they paid off because they had the know-how in the first place – which, until the advent of T.V., made people prefer movies to any other form of entertainment.

Why were American films international? As I've tried to point out, because innately the American is international. But there is another, less immediately discernible reason – censorship. The fear of offending censors, both national and stateside, as well as the endless Church and women's organizations that spring up at the slightest hint of scandal, loomed large in Hollywood, creating a universally acceptable product. The tools needed to keep the censors at bay and at the same time avoid baby talk in the film were as delicate as those of a Swiss watchmaker. The use of double-entendre to suggest what could not and, anyway, need not be depicted to make a point; wit and pace to speed over shallow situations that either would not stand analysis or would be censorable if treated straightforwardly – a general air of unreality which was created by the stars, who could by their presence in a role, suggest by personality what would have been cut if spoken. One law may have been good for all of Germany or France or Italy or England – but the United States was too diverse and made up of too many different ethnic groupings with indigenous moral outlooks who settled in, and dominated, certain states and whose state laws reflected their differing social and economic backgrounds and interests. Though based on the principles of the Bill of Rights, the local state laws differed in a number of points from state to state, and each had its own censorship-boards to guard against infractions. The New Englanders were more puritanical than their West Coast cousins; Southerners were more racially conscious, proud and stubborn. The cinema, to reach the all-American market, had to attain an acceptable level for all. Once it achieved that it was only natural that it should be equally acceptable to European audiences.

For a film to reach its widest possible market, it had to be ethnically unrecognizable regardless of plot, characters and situations although ethnic aspects served to add a tinge of reality, and it had not to collide with the many 'do nots' laid down by the censors. As I said

Francesca Bertini, Isa Miranda, Silvana Mangano, Gina Lollobrigida, Sophia Loren.

ROMANCE AND REALISM

Hollywood's *Mata Hari* (1932) with Garbo.
The realistic French treatment with Jeanne Moreau as *Mata Hari, Agent 821* (1965).

***Algiers* with Charles Boyer and Hedy Lamarr.**
***Pepe Le Moko* (1936) – again the realism came from France, the romance from Hollywood.**

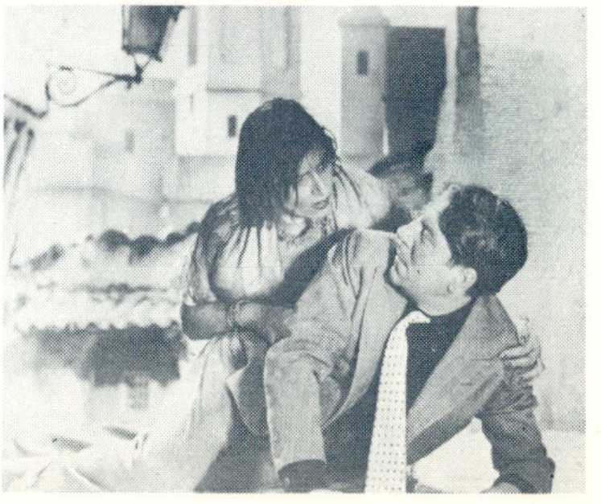

earlier, the result was – at its best – the success of sophisticated, glamorous, marvellously inventive, albeit artificial, films throughout the world.

Whenever in the history of the American Cinema a point was reached when it became a matter of maturing or losing the audience, the heads of studios managed to put off the fateful decision by the discovery of 'sound', 'colour', 'wide screen', '3D'. But finally movies could no longer escape reality with sleights of hand which had become pathetic. Whatever the reason for the introduction of sound, the outcome was a vigorous, healthy and adventurous new medium even though one which was used to further the same old delusions. But such latter-day gimmicks as the 'smellies' were the ineffectual wiles of a waning industry. It became an economic necessity for the American cinema to come to terms with what audiences of the 60s and 70s regarded as an acceptable reality. But for the first half of this century, it had managed to show life as it could be lived in the imagination: it was a magic mystery box and so far there has been nothing to replace it.

In the late 50s Russia exported a series of films to the West that presented a warmer, less doctrinaire view of Eastern Europe than had been seen before.

No book on romance can be written without bringing in the works of Max Ophuls, Willi Forst, Josef von Sternberg and King Vidor. But one will also include works of men who have specialized in the romantic genre without always gaining the same recognition for their talents. Directors like Douglas Sirk, Mario Soldati, David Miller, Joseph Pevney, John Cromwell, Gregory La Cava, Clarence Brown and John M. Stahl made some of the classics of the genre. Above all, Frank Borzage, master of the romantic cinema, was one of the great poet-entertainers to work in Hollywood.

There are other and perhaps truer definitions of romance, and who can say for sure what is, and what is not, romantic. One man's lover may be another's anathema. Though cowboys have been known to kiss their horses, and Lassie affectionately licks his master's face, unless it can be certified as a case of beauty and the beast, you will not find it here. Louis Pasteur may have made hearts skip a beat and pulses race with his discoveries, but if he is not shown to have been inspired by the love of Mrs Pasteur, you will have to look for him elsewhere – whereas M. and Mme Curie, immortalized by Greer Garson and Walter Pidgeon, fall into my heading as a romantic team. Women who do not hesitate to walk the streets to earn money with which to feed their children and buy the medicine to save their husbands, even though their actions will be misunderstood by those they love best till the end; the noble mother who finds herself on trial for murder and refuses to give her name so her grown children's happiness will not be ruined, these are the makers of movie legends. Finally, if you have not already guessed, it is not life, but the imitation of life, the 'once upon a time . . .' that constitutes romance in the cinema.

Jean Harlow – her presence suggested what no censor could cut.

Danielle Darrieux in *Le Plaisir* – an image that is the distillation of Romantic Cinema at its best.

CHAPTER TWO

GODS & GODDESSES

PART 1: GODS AND GODDESSES

The movie's greatest contribution to romance has been the close-up. Without it there would be no stars as we know them to-day, and, without them, the romantic cinema would not exist.

While some directors, notably King Vidor, Frank Borzage, von Sternberg and Max Ophuls have turned to romantic themes for their greatest works, it is the star who serves as the guide for any appreciation of the romantic cinema, and it was around the stars and their times that much of the romantic cinema revolved. M.G.M., symbol of Hollywood, built up their women stars and specialized in creating vehicles for them. A history of the films of a star like Garbo or Crawford is in itself a chart of the romantic cinema.

Birgitte Helm in *City of Song*.

Any list of romantic personalities is bound to be limited to those I have seen and to whom I've responded; to be fair to all the movie idols would need the kind of book which this cannot hope to be. My choice of stars is limited by personal tastes built up in an impressionable age but which have not changed over the years. My fascination for one actress began with a collection of yellowing photos that fell into my hands. Among them I discovered a face that enchanted me: the captivating Nancy Carroll, whose infectious laughter often hid so movingly the dilemmas that beset her heroines. I still remember the first shot of an English talkies vamp, Betty Stockfield, seen, I recall, in profile among the ruins of a Roman amphitheatre in a very early musical called *City of Song* that served primarily to unleash the unruffling features of tenor Jan Kiepura on feminine hearts throughout Europe. In that moment, she looked indescribably beautiful and exotic until the camera closed in and she talked – the ruin of many an English beauty. I was later to discover that for the long shots they had kept the star of the German version (shot simultaneously to cut costs), and that architectural profile really belonged to one of the screen's archetypal femmes fatales, the German Brigitte Helm.

Regrettably, I have seen too few of the continental favourites of the silent era – the Danish vamp Betty Nansen, the American Fern Andra who was a star in German silent films, Mia May, or the Countess Agnes Esterhazy among others of the hugely popular German stars of the silent era. I know even less first hand about the early Italian divas who, in rare stills, can be seen entangled in their own mortal coils resulting from their excessive abandon to temptation. Descriptions of these ladies and their vehicles by those who saw and fell victim to the charms of such femmes fatales as Lyda Borelli, Francesca Bertini, and the gaunt, sloe-eyed Pina Mellichelli, make this an omission one would like to correct. The great Italian goddess of the 30s and 40s was the beautiful Isa Miranda, star of Max Ophuls's *La Signora di Tutti* ('32). *Zaza* ('42) and *Malombra* ('42) are among her more glamorous successes made during the Fascist regime by directors (Castellani and Soldati) who took refuge in classicism to avoid involvement in the country's politics.

Fern Andra
A switch from the old routine – she came from America to become a star in Germany.

I wish, too, I knew more about the films and the stars of the countries behind the Iron Curtain, for those who have made it to American shores included the beauteous Russian Anna Sten; the ornate Hungarians from Vilma Banky on through Illona Massey,

Miliza Korjus to Zsa Zsa Gabor – never quite to be taken seriously, but decorative in many films – and some other attractive stars of which the most famous was undoubtedly Poland's Pola Negri. And Sweden: any country that can export such screen legendaries as Viveca Lindfors, Ingrid Bergman and Greta Garbo, Marta Toren and Zarah Leander – and the whole Bergman trophy-room of heroines – merits a keener look than I have been able to take. But the Swedes have always intrigued us. And this list does not even begin to mention the men.

The marvel, the magic of those early stars was that the less we knew about them, the easier it was for us to believe the outrageous claims that were made for them. Knowledge is a good thing for dealing with the real world, but what purpose does it serve the imagination? It may in part be dependent on the things around it but is not limited by it. Hollywood's great gift was that it allowed each one of us to dream in our own way, unimpeded by reality.

The star who projected an image of himself by living it and succumbing to it himself was only doing what kings did who believed in their divine rights in order to convince the people that they had such rights and thus maintain their station and their hold on the people. They *looked* imposing in order to *be* imposing. It is a corollary of the civilized principle that we have always judged a man by what he wears. The more festive and important the occasion, the more brilliant the robes of the priests and vice-versa. Sadly for stars, unlike those former monarchs, their faith in themselves is based on a slightly more sophisticated public's interest in them as types rather than individuals, so that their existence as stars (though, sad for them, not always their faith in themselves) ceases when the public has lost interest. And a star without a public is sadder than a king without a country (cf. Norma Desmond in *Sunset Boulevard* and Mae Murray's autobiography 'The Self Enchanted'). It is true that names, once great, cease to have any power over us. Even when it so happens that we continue to admire what our forefathers admired, our admiration is either conventional, perfunctory or based on other reasons than theirs!

Whatever appeal we may find today in the bizarre goings-on in the Hollywood of the 20s and 30s, it is not the same as theirs. We can marvel and gasp at the audacity and panache of their outrageous gestures, such as the cable Gloria Swanson was supposed to have sent to Paramount's Adolph Zukor. Prior to her return from France with a print of her film and a newly acquired Marquis husband, she commandingly cabled: 'arrange ovation'. Though she always denied sending it, the gesture was certainly in keeping with the more extravagant behaviour of the stars of the time. What stars today, more sophisticated and more conservative, would dare to indulge in any of the wild flights of behaviour that were a common occurrence in the Hollywood of the 20s when everything was done for the first time and every star created his own image by trial and error as he went along?

A lot of what one reads and hears about the things stars did and the way they lived seems naïve and bizarre today, but the early stars had a style and reckless imagination that not only carried themselves in its

Illona Massey.
Zarah Leander.
Isa Miranda.
Mia May.
Lilian Harvey.

wake, but swept the world. They were foolish, they were extravagant, too many of them lived for the day and failed to see the end ahead but, in that, there was the breath of romance. The western star, Tom Mix, had a neon light over his house to let the world know where he lived, and his initials were monogrammed on everything he owned, including his horse and saddle. The 'orchidacious' Corinne Griffith's bathroom with all its gold-plated fixtures rivalled any set in Cecil B. De Mille films. Today Richard Burton gives Liz Taylor diamonds, a gesture that reminds one of the extravagance of yesteryear when Joseph M. Schenck gave a forty-storey apartment building to his film-star wife, Norma Talmadge, to celebrate their eighth wedding anniversary in 1924. Today these are part of the mad and amusing history of films. Then they riveted millions of film-goers to whom such behaviour was part of the image they had of films and the people who made them.

They had to be young to become stars. It took not only desperate will to aim for something so illusory, but also the energy and strength of youth to try and turn it into reality. And among the galaxy, the romantic stars shone the brightest and left an impact that imprinted itself on the daily life of their generation.

PART 2: SILENT STARS

It was the public who first made film companies aware that there was money in the faces featured in their films. The producers may not have welcomed the idea with open arms, perhaps foreseeing the time when stars would become the most powerful and often the most expensive single part of a film. But they could not ignore the fact that money was to be made by giving the public what it wanted. The Biograph Co. was among the first to learn this when exhibitors and movie-goers alike wrote to request more films with, and information about, the leading lady they had dubbed 'The Biograph Girl' for want of any other means of identification. Till then no-one had thought it necessary to identify the actors in the films. Florence Lawrence, a pretty blonde with some previous stage experience, was thus the first star of American movies, though her popularity was soon eclipsed by a flood of new faces. That was in 1908.

By 1914, Mary Pickford, Blanche Sweet, Clara Kimball Young, the mature matinée idol Maurice Costello, and Francis X. Bushman (whose profile rivalled Barrymore's and who became the first male sex-symbol in the movies) were only a handful of the many names that sold tickets. But to Theda Bara goes the distinction of making the press-agent an integral instrument in the fabric of Hollywood. For, beginning with her, outrageous legends were concocted to further the box-office appeal of her films. Stories that would outlast many of the stars who had inspired them in the first place became part of film history, though perhaps never again were they able to be quite so outrageously splendid in their make-believe as those about Theodosia Goodman, demure daughter of Middle America, who gazed at a captive audience from across the sand-bleached bones of the men she had vamped to destruction.

THE BRITISH STYLE

The English have provided the movies with some cool, ladylike beauties such as Madeleine Carroll, Valerie Hobson and Deborah Kerr. A different type was Margaret Lockwood, the unrivalled queen of British cinema's romantic sex dramas of the 40s, usually with a demoniac James Mason as her consort. More serene beauties were Phyllis Calvert, Patricia Roc and Celia Johnson, partnered by Stewart Granger, John Mills and Michael Wilding.

Trevor Howard and Celia Johnson in *Brief Encounter* (1946), everyone else's idea of the perfect little British picture, all restraint and tea cups.

Madeleine Carroll.

Stewart Granger in *Caravan* (1946).

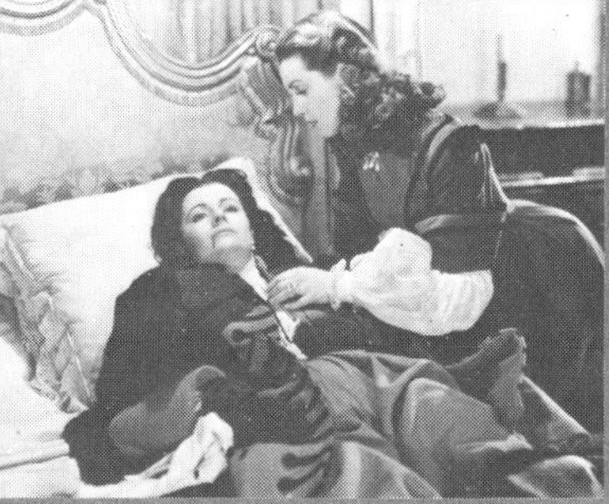

Margaret Lockwood and Patricia Roc in *The Wicked Lady* (1945).

An ominous James Mason in *The Man In Grey* (1943).

THE FRENCH STYLE

The French have their bevy of provocative romantics like Micheline Presle; the worldly, prestigious Edwige Feuillere, who did not mind baring her breasts in the pursuit of her art; the spiritual, blonde idol of the French, Michele Morgan, and the pubescent, carnal Brigitte Bardot.

Micheline Presle and Gerard Philippe in ***Le Diable Au Corps*****, the film which started Philippe on his rise to stardom. He excelled by virtue of his striking good looks and the intelligence he brought to his roles. His romantic appeal lay in his presence rather than in his roles – and in the dreams of his audience. He exerted on the public the same spell he cast over the heroines in his films.**

Michele Morgan in ***Quai Des Brumes*****. Anouk Aimee as** ***Lola*****. Edwige Feuillere in** ***The Eagle Has Two Heads*****. Brigitte Bardot and Christian Marquand in** ***And God Created Woman*****.**

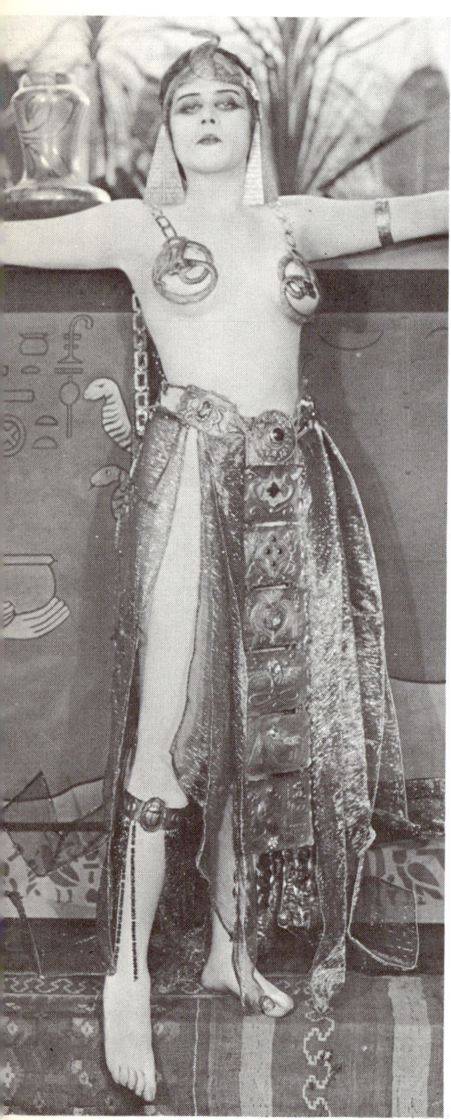

To be an outcast from decent society, with death the only hope, was the standard fee extracted by Victorian morality for those who strayed from the straight and narrow path to follow the way of all flesh, the lust that knows no love and is all consuming. While England, to whom Americans looked for their examples, had shed the Victorian inhibitions with the Queen's death in 1901, a large section of America insisted on a puritan sexual repressiveness, and believed in the Lord of the Israelites as thumped at them by the travelling evangelists scouring the Midwest for souls to bring to salvation. The crowds they attracted to the Lord were the stuff of which the vamp's public was made.

So, what more ideal a subject for that purple proselytizing than the screen's first love goddess – purgatory's ivory angel, The Vamp. Overnight Theda Bara became one of Hollywood's brightest stars (a much abused claim but true in this case) with the release of her first feature film *A Fool There Was.* No star before her and very few after, except Rudolph Valentino and Mae West, became so widely known in such a short space of time. When the film was released in January 1915 few people had heard of her. By June of that year, thanks to her demoniac roles, she was the baleful red star in a constellation of pretty, white luminaries. The reasons leading up to her success and the legends concocted about her are the stuff that musicals are made of. The Fox Company, new on the scene and eager to advance as a major film-making organization, had acquired the screen-rights to the stage-play inspired by Kipling's poem 'The Vampire' – 'a rag, a bone and a hank of hair' – which in turn had been inspired by a painting by Burne-Jones. The role was first offered to Virginia Pearson, who had created it on the stage. When she and several others, including Alice Hollister who had already starred in a film called *The Vampire* the year before and who specialized in that sort of role, refused, Fox decided to give it to an unknown whom Edward Jose, the film's male lead, had seen in a small bit in *The Stain.* In other stories it was director Frank Powell who asked for her. The young actress with the stage-name Theodosia de Coppet accepted the role at a very modest 100 dollars a week (compare this to the 2,000 dollars a week Fox paid the Danish actress Betty Nansen, who had created the 'Vamp' archetype in European films, when they signed her). *A Fool There Was* became the box-office hit of January 1915. Theda's price went up.

Now began the most preposterous and amusing build-up in film history – as much a part of the romance of films as Theda herself. A newspaperman, Al Selig, was signed to take care of her image, and the first thing he ordered was a change of name. To quote Terry Ramsaye in his history of Hollywood's early years, 'A Million and One Nights':

'De Coppet did not appeal to Fox, who was seeking something that would decorate the billboards. And a siren called Theodosia Goodman was out of the question – that sounded too much like the hapless victim of a Vamp. The actress was consulted for the choice of her name. Theda Bara was her suggestion. For "de Bara" had been the name of her maternal grandmother. Theda was merely the family abbreviation of Theodosia, her real name. (She was probably born in

1890, but never revealed her true age, which started another tradition.) So, Theda Bara it was.

'Thereupon it ordained a career of vampiring screen sin for the (privately) demure and circumspect Miss Theodosia Goodman. Her first success was an encouragement to greater iniquities of fiction. Immediately Miss Goodman began to acquire a most amazing atmospheric past. Her press agents plied the motion picture columns of the press with the announcement that Theda Bara was the daughter of a French artist and his Arabian mistress, born on the sands of the Sahara in the shade of the Sphynx. Bara was, the publicists said, a mere Baconian anagram, being Arab spelled backwards. This proved the rest of the story. Meanwhile Theda was just a mere re-arrangement of the letters of death. This deadly Arab girl was a crystal-gazing seeress of occult powers, wicked as fresh red paint, and as poisonous as dried spiders. The stronger the copy grew, the more it was printed. Stills depicting her in poses even more bizarre than some of her films flooded the country. One such took advantage of her interests in the occult (cards and horoscopes mostly) by showing her peering intently over the sarcophagus of an Egyptian King in the Metropolitan Museum of Art and finding familiar traits in the mummy's face. In all of them her eyes were kohl-rimmed (creating a mad craze for mascara among the women) and her full lips a livid scarlet in a large white face so that it looked as if all the blood in her head had concentrated in her mouth. When not gazing enticingly from the photogravure sections of magazines, she would have a bitter-sweet, melancholic smile suggesting a weariness such as no mortal woman could ever know.'

Even the interviewers who came to write about her for their magazines, though they knew better, went along with the studio's fiction. One of them said it all: 'When considering parabolic fire, vaccination, municipal politics and German cookery one must believe those facts which are most apparent. But women are not tangible, either as objects of reason or prophecy, and therefore he that hath wit will believe about them whatever pleases him most.

'For that reason I prefer to disbelieve those stupid people who insist that Theda Bara's right name is Theodosia Goodman, and that she is by, of and from Cincinnati. To those persons I put my fingers in my eyes and wink my ears. I wish to believe, I am going to believe, I do believe that Allah is Allah, and that Bara is Bara; that the ivory angel of purgatory is an Eastern Star, was born under the shadow of the Sphinx and in physical texture is as bizarre a woof of bloods as she is cosmopolitan in mentality.'

And he gave an example of the tribulations that beset a Daughter of the Sphinx in the streets of New York. Miss Bara told him, 'A terrible thing happened yesterday. I was walking near my home. I had a great big red apple in my hand, and ahead of me I spied a little girl with thin legs and oh, such a hungry look! I put my arms around her and put the apple in her hand. Her eyes fell on my face and a look of terror came into hers. "It's the Vampire!" She ran . . . I went home and sobbed like the littlest child.' The audiences thronging to see her films found that the heavy-lidded raven-haired image on the screen

Francesca Bertini – her languourous sensuality needed no time to find its mark.

An early Italian temptress in *Cabiria* (1914).

THEDA BARA

'The Vampire' or Vamp in the movie dictionary meant a lady of neither morals nor occupation – unless the destroying business could be called an occupation.

Some pale imitations of *the* Vamp, Seena Owen Valeska Surat Luise Glaum.

stood up to their expectations. 'Little shopgirls read about her and swallowed their gum with excitement. Every good little girl in the nation went to see Theda do on the screen those things which every good little girl would like to do, if she dared, now and then.'

Her reputation for sinning preceded her cross-country journey from New York to Los Angeles. Stopping off in Chicago to do some publicity work, Chicago's mayor and film censor declined to meet her. In her autobiography, Hollywood's columnist Louella Parsons recalled that distant press conference, which had been arranged to impress the press, and did. 'She received us in a darkened parlor, draped with black and red, in the tones of her sweeping gown. She was white, languid and poisonously polite. The air was heavy with tuberoses and incense. The staging worked magic. The interviews were in hushed tones, and the results were columns. When the door closed on the last caller the windows went up. "Give me air!" she commanded.'

Bara worked her willowy way through no less than forty pictures in her three years at Fox, of which today only one, her first, seems to be at all available, making her the most mysterious of all the great stars. In her films she alternated between all-out sirens and demure heroines; both were successful, but so strong was the public's identification of her with the former that they suspected her motivations as the latter. As Bara herself explained in an early interview: 'I like the adventuress because she has colour and intensity. Do you understand? I can make something out of her. She stands forth vivid and living. She is the only human sort of woman the American public wants; they must have colourless heroines, or sugar-sweet heroines, playing white little parts in white little love stories. I am not saying that American women are like that; they are warm, wonderful vital things, but people seem to want heroines and not women. Therefore I choose to play wicked women, because when photoplay women are good and real they often cease to be women.'

In her understanding of the demands of the type-casting system even if not through the roles she played, she bridges the gap to the more complex 'femmes fatales' and 'love goddesses' the American public would demand soon after her retirement in 1919.

There were screen vamps before Bara, like the more mortal Italian divas. Although they also spent a great deal of their time writhing about in sexy, provocative poses, they differed from their American cousin in sophistication and inasmuch as they were as partial to the human lusts they aroused as their victims were and usually died with them. Bara was an object of desire in herself and needed to do little more than look and smile wickedly for the hero to throw up his home, family and children for another just like it. There would be numerous second-string vamps during her brief but never dull career, but none ever reached her stature. She began as a star and retired as one. Like all the great love goddesses she was original, and that made her singular. Unlike the heroines of her films, her private life was remarkably unsensational, and exceptionally happy. She made and kept a great deal of the money she earned. Soon after her retirement in 1919 (though she did attempt several comebacks in the 20s before she finally stopped) she married the director of some of her films, Charles Brabin. When she died of cancer in 1955, they were still together. And, in that, she was probably unique as well.

Between the two extremes, the heroines of Griffith's films exemplified by Lillian Gish – pale cheeks, fluttery lids and trembling hands forever supplicating some unheeding grace to save them – and Theda Bara, the American cinema came of age in time for the next decade. It was only a few years away but a lifetime in attitudes. And with it came the sheiks and the flappers, the women of the world and the boys next door.

What Bara had meant to her public, Rudolph Valentino meant to his. As much a prisoner of the image that gave Valentino his extraordinary success as had been the Vamp to Bara, 'The Sheik' – the name derived from the title of his most famous role – became a noun and an adjective to describe the kind of loving that girls dreamed of. The men of the day emulated Valentino as several decades later they would James Dean. His appeal responded to the more relaxed libido of the war-liberated era he dominated. Valentino would be emulated by a host of imitators but never eclipsed – although there were intimations that his career was on the wane by the time of his untimely death from peritonitis in 1926. His last two films, *The Eagle* and *Son of the Sheik*, benefited enormously from a frenzy of necrophiliac affection for the star who was no more.

It was Valentino's casting for the coveted role of Julio in *The Four Horsemen of The Apocalypse* that helped turn a struggling young actor and dancer into a star. But it was as the savagely brutal but honourable lover riding the desert as the hero of E. M. Hull's best-selling novel, loosely inspired by the front-page exploits of the romantic Englishman living and fighting with the desert tribesmen – Lawrence of Arabia – that Valentino became a legend.

The story was a pure and very simple romantic fabrication. The cast – haughty English Lady, Diana Mayo; masterful desert prince, Sheik Ahmed Ben Hassan and oily, lecherous villain Omair, could have been the ingredients of a rollicking musical (Sigmund Romberg's 'The Desert Song' used pretty much the same formula). With the haughty maid threatening to kill herself rather than submit to a man's will, and a thousand desert warriors led by the Sheik riding to rescue her from the ignoble villain, one wonders how the 'hip' Fitzgerald generation could have taken any of this seriously. But what made *The Sheik* was its star. Medium height, trimly built – his body kept in shape by daily two-hour workouts – slick cap of hair, and beautiful face, Valentino had an undeniably potent sex-appeal. His humourless intensity fired his portrayals with moody conviction. In desert robes or evening suits, as the bewigged and powdered *Monsieur Beaucaire*, or as the doomed matador of Vincente Blasco Ibanez's bullfight classic, *Blood and Sand*, Valentino appealed to the most basic erotic desires in his public, especially the women. It was not friendship or understanding, not security or equality that they idolized Valentino for; it was his sexual magnetism. Like his leading ladies, they might have gasped, they might have trembled and thrown their hands up over their face as he tore into their chambers, but they

RUDOLPH VALENTINO
in *Blood and Sand* **(1922).** *Monsieur Beaucaire* **(1924).** *Son Of The Sheik* **(1925).** *The Sheik* **(1921).**

PHOTOPLAY
25 cents

SCREENLAN

CINEMA
THE MAGAZINE OF THE PHO

PHOTOPLA
DECEMBER
The
Beauty Who Sits Alo

JULY
25¢
CLASSIC

MOTION PICTUR
DECEMBER – 25 CTS
Fighting the Lean Years

PHOTOPLAY
OCTOBER
Whose Heart is Whose
in Hollywood

PHOTOPLA
"When Ten Cents Was Big Money"
How To Hold Your You

Motion Picture
Classic
25

PICTURE PLAY
NOV. 1927
LITTLE JOURNEYS TO FILMLAND
The Truth About Salar

CINEMA
THE MAGAZINE OF THE PHOTOPLAY

otion Picture
25 CENTS
The Talkies
First Birth

The National Guide to Motion Pictures
PHOTOPLAY
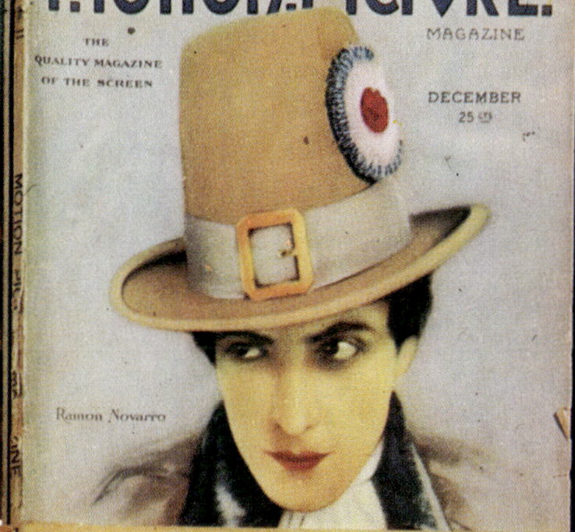
MOTION PICTURE
MAGAZINE
THE QUALITY MAGAZINE OF THE SCREEN
DECEMBER
Ramon Novarro

TION PICTURE
QUALITY MAGAZINE OF THE SCREEN
MAGAZINE
1 Shilling

The World's Leading Moving Picture Magazine
PHOTOPLAY
The Studio Secret
The Tragedies of Pauline Frederick
VALENTINO'S HOLLYWOOD LIFE

MOTION PICTURE
MAY
MAGAZINE
Gloria Swanson

would have submitted. Few of his films were especially distinguished by the intelligence of either subject or treatment and *The Sheik* even less so, but it remains his best-loved and remembered role because the motivations of his part were the least complex.

The publicity hand-outs for the film inflamed imaginations:

'He wanted only one thing and she knew what it was, and it would be only a matter of time before he got it.

"Who are you?" she gasped.

"I am the Sheik Ahmed Ben Hassan."

'She was trapped, powerless, defenseless. It was inevitable; there was no help to be expected, no mercy to be hoped for. With a start of recollection she realized fully whose arm was round hers and whose breast her head was resting on. Her heart beat with a sudden violence. What was the matter with her? Why did she not shrink from the pressure of his arm and the contact of his warm, strong body? What had happened to her? Quite suddenly she knew – knew that she loved him, that she had loved him for a long time, even when she thought she hated him and when she fled from him. Love had come to her at last, she who had scorned it so fiercely. The men who had loved her had not had the power to touch her, she had given love to no one, she had thought that she could not love . . .'

John Barrymore in 'THE BELOVED ROGUE'

Sean Connery in the 60s trend in ***Diamonds Are Forever*****.**

'In my day we all had faces . . .' Gloria Swanson. Some of the faces that filled the screen and the fan magazines in the 20s and 30s.

There it was in a nutshell. It was the sort of story the film studios loved because they could be faithful to the original with little head scratching for deeper meanings, or wondering if it was simple enough for the great public to grasp. With a confidence that did not go unrewarded they wrote '*The Sheik* is a motion picture de luxe, colourful, vivid, enthralling, thrilling, romantic, produced at tremendous expense for your delight. It is a picture of tremendous heart appeal, faithfully adapted from the book. To miss it is to miss one of the greatest pictures of all time.'

No actor since the early days of Douglas Fairbanks had so captured the public's fancy. What distinguished Valentino from his many imitators was the common sense which came across in the interviews he gave when studio press-agents were not around to watch what he said. He talked freely to anyone interested in printing what he thought and not what they thought their readers might want to hear. On the subject of new Valentinos he first asked what every subsequent 'symbol' would echo about themselves in the same dilemma: 'What is a Valentino? I don't know. In *The Four Horsemen* I played the role of Julio; in *Camille* I was Armand. In *The Sheik* or those other pictures, I didn't know who I was. In *Blood and Sand* I played Gallardo. But what is the role of Valentino? Perhaps a Valentino is simply Jesse Lasky's nightmare.' (Lasky was then the head of Paramount.) And he seemed ruefully amused about the numerous claims of people to have discovered him after his feverish rise to fame. 'Everybody except the person who did, claims to have discovered me. But when I think of some of the awful pictures I made in my past I wonder that anyone thinks it a credit to them to have discovered me.'

Prior to his role in *Four Horsemen* he had been a freelancer in a number of films, mostly as the heavy. June Mathis, then one of Hollywood's most important screenwriters, saw him playing a heavy in the popular Clara Kimball Young film, *Eyes of Youth* (1919). Miss Mathis had a great deal to do with putting *The Four Horsemen* together for Metro and making it one of the classics of the silent cinema and the foundation of the studio. She also selected a little-known Irish director, Rex Ingram, and a beautiful brunette, who became popular as a blonde, Alice Terry, as the leading lady. The film's world-wide fame and success established all concerned, but none more so than Valentino whose Julio seemed to step from the pages of the Ibanez novel. The three (director and stars) quickly followed this up with another success, *The Conquering Passion*.

Valentino consolidated his success as Armand in Nazimova's *Camille*, during which he met his bossy second wife, Natacha Rambova, who was the artistic designer of many of Nazimova's films. As soon as he had divorced his first wife, Jean Acker, also a friend of the eccentric Russian-born star, he married Natacha. He then left Metro for Paramount and *The Sheik*, but was soon fighting Paramount in the courts to break his contract. While this kept him off the screen at a time when the public clamour for him was overwhelming, he and his wife went on a coast-to-coast vaudeville tour as exhibition dancers, doing the tango at an estimated fee of 6,000 dollars a week. During his absence, and even after his death, it seemed as if South America's male population was on the move to Hollywood, for almost every type of star took a turn at 'sheiking'. Even the sentimental boy-next-door, Charles Farrell, played a dusky sheik in *Fazil*; and the reserved, donnish Milton Sills also got on a horse to sweep a willing maiden into his arms and off into the desert. Sheiks became an epidemic. When Natacha gave Valentino a slave bracelet, which he wore on his wrist to show his devotion to her, every dime-store soda-jerk 'sheik' across the nation would be sure to wear one. They emulated his patent-leather hair style and the languour of his poses and his love-making in the back seats of their jalopies, which had to serve for cushioned, perfumed tents. Threatening to become endemic, there were editorial outcries over what 'powder puffs' young clean American boys were being turned into by these foreign Lotharios. But Valentino's fans stayed faithful while his imitators gave way.

Valentino was born in Italy in 1895 of a French mother and an Italian father. He arrived in New York in 1913 when he was 18 and made a living as a gigolo, dancing in cafés. Women were said to have shot husbands for him. A woman made him a star. Women, judging from his domineering second wife and his last love, Pola Negri, also dominated his private life. And it was women, 50,000 strong, who stopped the traffic outside the funeral home in New York where his body lay in state after his death. They fainted, became hysterical, and a couple of the more impressionable even killed themselves rather than go on living in a world with no hope of any more Valentino films to fill their waking dreams.

Besides Valentino's undeniably erotic attraction for American and Anglo-Saxon women, founded to some degree on the myth that Latins were hot lovers, Valentino differed from the stereotype which time and distance has made of him in other ways. He possessed a streak of vulnerability that would bring the heroine to his bedside at

the first sight of a scratch, and he conducted himself with a sense of honour that won men's respect, if not their enthusiastic endorsement. In *Cobra* he refused to succumb to the vamping of Nita Naldi because she was his best friend's wife, yet he later shields her reputation when she is killed in a hotel fire, thereby losing both his friend and his own girl. In *The Sheik* he combined the appeal of the brutal savage lover with the sensibilities of the civilized man.

Invariably there came a point in his films when he had to undress – whether getting in or out of the suit of gold worn by the matador; bedecked in ropes of jewels and pearls and not much else, as *The Young Rajah*, or as the marquis pretending to be a hairdresser to find true love in *Monsieur Beaucaire*, which contains one of the most elaborate scenes of a man's toilet on the screen. There were always scenes to expose his physique.

Two male physiques in the silent cinema still arouse admiration today. Two actors – the lithe and feline Valentino and the gymnastic, bouncing 'Vitamin Kid', Douglas Fairbanks Sr. Fairbanks was in a class of his own when it came to leaping over rooftops, onto horses' backs, sliding down a sail, or doing battle with 40 adversaries. But his athletic prowess usually finished at the bedroom door, whereas one could see Valentino moving, supple and silent from alcove to bedroom, in and out of boudoirs. Fairbanks's superb body was cultivated to carry out unrivalled stunts; Valentino cultivated his body for narcissistic delights which he was not averse to sharing.

Like Valentino, Douglas Fairbanks invariably undressed, yet the act carried no major sexual significance, not even when, as *The Thief of Baghdad*, he steals into the bed-chamber of the princess with the grace of a ballet dancer and the honour of a boy scout. The difference between the two men is the difference between the circus artist and the bedroom artist.

The emphasis on masculine pulchritude was in evidence throughout the 20s. While women flattened their breasts to emulate a boy's slimness, the men stood semi-nude in films where heroes like Richard Dix and George O'Brien played noble savages. This phase faded out by the end of the decade but came back into prominence with Alan Ladd's arrival in the 40s. He invariably stripped off for brandings, whippings, or sometimes simply a change of shirt. Whatever the ploy, the exposure of his physique was a staple of his films much as the scenes of undressing were in those of Valentino and Fairbanks. Though most male sex-symbols invariably show off their biceps, the prominent display of the body was one of the main attractions of Valentino's films and in that sense he was not to have an equal until the Warhol super-star of today, Joe Dallesandro.

Ramon Novarro, who displayed more of his body than any other actor of his day, did it with the grace and joy of a Shepherd King, whom he suggested. If Fairbanks was King Arthur and Valentino was Lancelot, Novarro, with his choir-boy face, was Sir Galahad. Our first sight of him in *Ben Hur* comes as an iris slowly opens up on the dark screen to show a dove lovingly pecking Novarro's lips. In that single image one can see the strong connection between Novarro and other gentle heroes of Christian and Arthurian legend. He was already a popular favourite among the current crop of Latin lovers (few of whom were Latin and, judging from the stories that went around, not many of them were much as lovers either). He had been discovered by Rex Ingram who was looking for a replacement for Valentino when he was casting *The Prisoner of Zenda* and found in the young Mexican bit-player the grace and appearance he sought for Rupert of Hentzau. Be that as it may, *Ben Hur*, released in 1926, was the apex of Novarro's romantic career even though he continued to star well into the sound era. It was obvious in the grimly realistic style of the 30s that he was out of his time. The new brand of hero was tougher. The Gables, the Cagneys and the Rafts took what they wanted where they found it. Where Novarro would tremble fitfully with incipient passion and look mooningly at the shut door of the heroine's sleeping quarters, a Cagney wouldn't hesitate to rough her up, slap her down, and crash in any door locked to him. But in the romantic atmosphere that pervaded the 20s, a sleek-haired gigolo could become the romantic ideal by flaring his nostrils like a highly strung horse. The boyish qualities Novarro brought to his roles touched a maiden's heart. In that sense his appeal, though more exotic, was similar to the American 'apple pie' heroes played so well and so appealingly by Richard Barthelmess, ever since his great success as the shy back-woods dreamer of Joseph Hergesheimer's *Tolable David* (1921).

A newly formed company M.G.M., soon to become the first film studio of the world, had been responsible for *Ben Hur*. They had two other block-busters released the year before, Erich von Stroheim's highly personal version of *The Merry Widow* and King Vidor's *The Big Parade*, an unsentimental view of World War I, seen mostly through the eyes of its young hero, Jim Apperson. The heroes of both these films were played by the rapidly rising new favourite, John Gilbert. With Valentino's death, Gilbert took over as the number-one heart-throb. His ardour, his impetuosity, and devil-may-care virility were the material of which heroes were made, and these qualities are still as arresting when seen for the first time today. The youthful impatience in his love-making had a sincerity that would be equally at home in contemporary love stories. He conveyed feelings with a minimum of the moping looks that passed for love at a time when title writers were there to cover glazed stares with passionate captions. Gilbert's eyes sparkled, his lips rarely hid his teeth for long, a smile was always to hand. His wavy black hair fell endearingly across his forehead when he was carried away by his emotions instead of sticking to his scalp like the oily patent-leather cap, then the rage among college kids and Latin lovers. He stood straight, had a good body and was striking in clothes, especially uniforms, without looking like a clothes horse. And he was a good, albeit a limited, actor.

Gilbert's film career had begun unspectacularly back in 1916 when he took turns playing bit-parts, working as a screen writer, sometimes directing small-budget films and later as the star of a series of programmes for the Fox studio. It was King Vidor who made him a star at M.G.M. Vidor, a man's man and an extraordinarily romantic director throughout his long and varied career, brought out Gilbert's

Douglas Fairbanks *The Thief of Baghdad* **(1924).**
Rudolph Valentino *Young Rajah* **(1922).**
Alan Ladd *Two Years Before The Mast* **(1946).**
Joe Dallessandro *Trash* **(1970).**

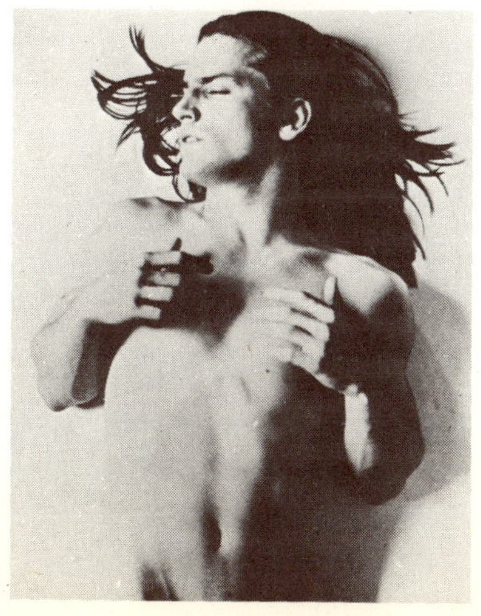

dichotomous appeal in a series of fine films that did much to establish them both. Besides *The Big Parade*, *La Bohême*, *Wife of the Centaur* and Bardley's *The Magnificent*, Vidor had first used him to advantage in Elinor Glynn's *His Hour* (1924). Gilbert played a Russian prince who fascinated, as well as terrified, a noble English lady (Aileen Pringle). And the movie consists mostly of the lady's pursuit by the prince. Like most of Vidor's work, the film is rich in romantic touches – in this case, a memorable sleigh-ride in which the two are buried up to their noses in furs, their breath forming a mist around their faces.

JOHN GILBERT
A romantic, idealistic, heroic rogue, he was every woman's master until he met Garbo; in her arms he became another man.

Gilbert's appeal lay in the contrast between the wolfish face he showed, which might have been thought to type him as a mustachio-twirling villain, and the sensibilities he displayed, in contrast to his looks. The dichotomy this created made him devilishly appealing.

From here on he became enormously popular and dominated the films in which he starred, yet he was also to become famous as half of one of the movies greatest love teams when the young Swedish Greta Garbo was given the female lead opposite him in *Flesh and The Devil* (1927). If he was slightly at sea as to how to respond to Lillian Gish's ethereal Mimi in *La Bohême*, elsewhere he was usually direct in his approach toward women and in charge of the romantic situation. But with Garbo he assumed a passive position, moving to the dictates of a will he could neither control nor resist. From the intensity of their love-scenes the public was convinced that the films they made together were nothing less than a thrilling invasion of privacy. They made only three films at the crest of their popularity – *Flesh and The Devil*, *Love* and *Woman of Affairs*, but their position as the greatest romantic couple in movies has never been challenged. At the time it was rivalled only by the serene, romantic wooing of the pictorially exquisite Vilma Banky by Ronald Colman, and by everybody's favourite young lovers, Janet Gaynor and Charles Farrell, who were climbing the stairs to their garret heavens. But Gilbert and Greta Garbo were singular. Garbo's forceful eroticism in their films only serves to heighten the appeal of Gilbert's reticence and sensibilities. In their love-scenes she is the active, he the passive agent. Her sexual needs appeared greater than his ability to fulfil them, and their love seemed based on passion and torment. The spell could only be broken by her death, so conforming to Hollywood's artificial romantic ideal. It was Europe (Garbo) confronting America (Gilbert) in a conflict between the two civilizations that runs through so much of American cinema.

At the height of the Garbo-Gilbert craze the studio was so eager to cash in on their initial success that Gilbert was brought in to replace another Latin lover of the period, Ricardo Cortez, who had meanwhile begun work opposite Garbo in an adaptation of Tolstoy's 'Anna Karenina'. With their eyes on the market, the studio felt that this would not be a suitable title to describe the momentous re-teaming of the lovers of the century. At a script-conference someone came up with the suggestion that it be called *Heat*. Frances Marion, who had written the screenplay, pointed out how this might sound on the billboards if they had 'Gilbert and Garbo in *Heat*'. So they called it *Love* instead, and added a happy ending. Instead of throwing herself under the wheels of the train, Anna re-appears at the end, five years later, at the Military Academy her son is attending and sees Vronsky. He inquires after her. 'What has happened? Why are you wearing black?' In this version it is Karenin and not Anna who dies.

Ramon Novarro in *Ben Hur* (1927).

Everything about Gilbert was so much bigger than life, his ability to live and to share his joy, his enormous successes – when they came; his marriages to five beautiful ladies, three of them stars in their own right, and his passionate on-screen relationship with Garbo. It was, therefore, natural that the collapse of his career should be as well known today – perhaps even better known than his accomplishments. A sequence of unfortunate factors coincided to ruin him: a bad script – *One Glorious Night* – that belonged to the days of *His Hour*, and not to the dawning era of breadlines and starvation, combined with the bad recording quality of the early talkies, which emacsulated his voice, so that it was certainly not suitable for ardent vocal love-making. The qualities that made him would re-appear in such disparate later stars as Clark Gable, Errol Flynn and Gerard Philipe. He died in 1936, almost forgotten by his fans who would, six years earlier, have lined the streets for his funeral in an outburst of hysteria not unlike the one they had reserved for Valentino.

Another great lover, John Barrymore, was then in the prime of his physical condition. He was acclaimed the greatest Hamlet of his generation. He preferred to specialize in roles that allowed him to disguise his handsome features for more bizarre make-up, characters like Dr Jekyll and Mr Hyde or Captain Ahab, but the movie public preferred him as a dashing, moody, romantic hero. With his famous profile, sharp as a razor and his talents under control, Barrymore's screen-presence was a fascinating mixture of Gilbert's rakishness, Fairbanks's athleticism, and Ronald Colman's sincerity in love-making, without his being as popular as any of them. A series of romantic costume-roles were tailored to take greater advantage of his physical charms than of his acclaimed acting talents; among them *Beau Brummel*, *Beloved Rogue*, *The Tempest* and the very decorative and swashbuckling version of *Don Juan*. The latter especially gave him an opportunity to display all his qualities at one point or another. Leaping up and down staircases like Fairbanks in the beautifully staged duel that climaxes the film; gaily dallying with the ladies of the court of the Borgias, including the poisonous Lucrezia, he finally spies and succumbs to the one unsullied flower at the court, the beautiful Mary Astor. Though at first he attempts to take her by force, she struggles for her honour, and finally faints in his arms, thereby affecting a noble about-face in the hero to the point where he later risks life and limb for her honour, eventually winning her by gentleness where force has failed.

John Barrymore with Camilla Horn in *Tempest* (1928).

The reserved gentlemanly charm of the English actor Ronald Colman, allied to his beautiful brooding features, was to project him to the heights of public favour in the sound era. In the mid-20s his career got off to a bright start that eventually took him to a position second only to that of Garbo. But his most romantic asset could not be brought out until talkies came. His unique position was unassailed until his retirement from films and never equalled by any other actor thereafter. In films like *A Tale of Two Cities, Lost Horizon, The Prisoner of Zenda* (one of many, but by far the finest version of Anthony Hope's Ruritanian romance) and others like *Random Harvest*, his face and his remarkable dreamy voice, which he used, not to convince but to enchant, made him the romantic personification of every woman's dream. Whether as father or lover, dissolute dreamer, or sophisticated idealist, as beggar-poet, or foreign legionnaire, he was a man of honour and a prince among men. It is only fitting that for three generations of movie-goers and for anyone who has read Dickens's *A Tale of Two Cities*, Sidney Carton's immortal last lines known by every schoolboy, 'It is a far, far better thing I do than I have ever done. It is a far, far, better place I go to than I have ever known' should conjure up a romantic gesture that was uniquely Colman's.

Who could guess that behind this raffish, passionate exterior there was a quiet gentleman with an English soul?

Lillian Gish selected the young Englishman for her leading man in *The White Sister* because he photographed Italian. He was established as a star in his own right when he made his most successful silent film, playing the noblest of the brothers in *Beau Geste* ('27). His romantic reputation in silent films rests primarily on the five films he made as a team with the beautiful blonde Hungarian, Vilma Banky.

They were lush, attractively mounted costume-dramas like *The Night of Love* ('27), *The Magic Flame* ('27) and *Two Lovers* ('28); a very successful World War I romance of a soldier returning from the front, now blind, who pretends to be able to see so he can send his beloved away to happiness with their best friend, *The Dark Angel* (as popular a tear-jerker when Goldwyn re-made it in the 30s); and a western, *The Winning of Barbara Worth* ('26), in which Colman is a dude engineer who vies with a cowboy for the hand of fair Barbara. (The cowboy was the lanky Gary Cooper, just beginning to make his name.) With few exceptions, long-lasting screen-teams are not known for their warm off-set relationships, though this in no way affected the chemistry that took place between such couples as MacDonald and Eddy, Astaire and Rogers, or Banky and Colman. On the other hand, couples who might have been expected to strike sparks on the screen as they seem to do in private, are usually no more – often less – interesting than conventional teamings. One only has to look at the films Paul Newman co-starred in with his fine actress wife, Joanne Woodward, or the co-starring of Janet Leigh and Tony Curtis – and even more surprisingly the huge vacuum of the Elizabeth Taylor and Richard Burton series, beginning with the decidedly limpid *Cleopatra* in which her scenes with Rex Harrison carried infinitely more fire, to see that this is true.

RONALD COLMAN
Colman and Vilma Banky in *Night Of Love* (1927) and *Magic Flame* (1927). The success of the Colman/Banky team was due to their blending as physical types – her finely moulded blonde loveliness and his romantic stillness – rather than to any kindred spark between them.

Alongside the men, the 20s produced a series of romantic heroines, some continuing with modifications in the moulds first set up by Gish and Bara, while others including some of the most flamboyant and attractive personalities of the era broke new ground for future types. Few more so than the imported siren, Pola Negri, a more adult version of Theda Bara; and, at the other extreme, the aggressively young and alive spirit of the era, Clara Bow. Between them, every possible type of romantic and exotic, domestic and foreign heroine flowered. From the bizarre Russian star Alla Nazimova, to the placid lady-like

RONALD COLMAN
as Sidney Carton in ***A Tale of Two Cities*** **(1936).**

Norma Talmadge, whose popularity in the 20s was second only to that of 'America's Sweetheart', Mary Pickford.

Pickford's sex appeal insofar as it played a minor part in her screen roles was not unlike that of her husband – the athletic Douglas Fairbanks. Like Pickford and Talmadge, a great star of the previous decade, Lillian Gish, the Duse of the silent screen, sailed into the 20s even more famous, graduating from the Griffith-inspired child-women to child-brides, but death or disaster still came to her rescue before physical relationships had to be faced. In this way she could display her unexcelled ability for conveying frenzy and terror (with more than a hint of sexual overtones) in most of her films, though rarely to such telling effect as in Griffith's *Broken Blossom* ('19). In her greatest success of the decade, *The White Sister* (which she bought and produced independently), a flood arrived just in time to save her from renouncing the vows freshly made to God and His church when her soldier sweetheart, presumed dead in the desert, returns to claim her. In the superb psychological western *The Wind* ('26), as a young bride taken from the city to live and face the solitary hardships of pioneer life, a wind-storm intervenes to slowly drive her mad after she has killed and buried the marauding villain who had attempted to rape her during her husband's lengthy absence. No matter how romantic the subject of her films, there was something about Miss Gish that transformed earthly love into an antiseptic, Pre-Raphaelite substitute. She only played a nun in one of her films, *The White Sister*, but invariably her heroines seemed to have given themselves over to some private order. She disseminated passion of the kind found in cloisters of Verdun, where penitent sisters flail their bodies to keep out temptation and succeed in wild erotic fantasies instead. Even when she played Mimi of *La Bohême*, a girl in the Parisian Latin Quarter, one still felt that a man's touch was to her like the blood on Lady Macbeth's hands – something that could never again be wiped clean. This was not much like the warm and loving seamstress of Murger's stories of life and love under the rooftops of Paris. By their implied repugnance to the physical act of love, Gish's heroines suggest, on deeper study of her films (and her career is remarkable for its high standard and frequent brilliance), a Freudian mixture of frigidity and nymphomania. On the most immediate level, *Way Down East*, *Orphans of The Storm*, *Romola* and others, her work gave glimpses of one of the most poetic stars to grace the screen. Miss Gish was so ethereal she could hardly bring herself to kiss John Gilbert during the making of *La Bohême*. But she was prevailed upon and went back for retakes, as she herself put it in her memoirs, with a certain distaste still in her mouth, 'Oh, dear, I've got to go through another day of kissing John Gilbert.'

Gish had her own ideas about the love-scenes between Mimi and Rodolphe, and in them lies the key to her attitude on the subject in all her films. 'It seemed to me that, if we avoided showing the lovers in a physical embrace, the scenes would build up suppressed emotion and be much more effective. But I reckoned without the exploitation M.G.M. had given John Gilbert as the "Great Lover". King Vidor agreed with me, but the front office demanded that we include love

CHILD WOMEN

Lillian Gish with Ronald Colman in *White Sister* (1923).

Mary Miles Minter, Pickford's greatest rival until scandal ruined her career, was one of the many girls in the Pickford manner.

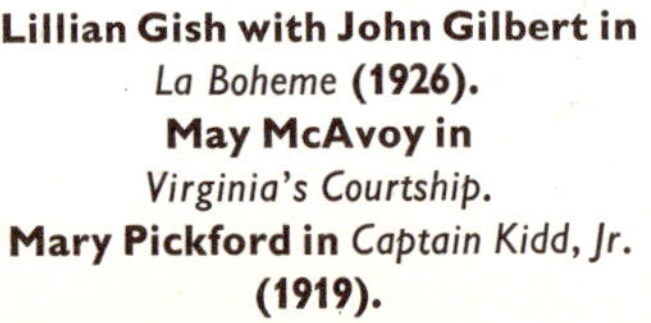

Lillian Gish with John Gilbert in *La Boheme* (1926).
May McAvoy in *Virginia's Courtship*.
Mary Pickford in *Captain Kidd, Jr.* (1919).

Janet Gaynor (1927).

Bessie Love

Lillian Gish

scenes.' Her death-scene was one of the most effective moments in a beautiful film. She was always excellent at renouncing the world or departing from life. Almost twenty years later and for the same director, her death-scene in *Duel in The Sun* with thunder and lightning flashing outside and the wind lashing at her rocking-chair on the verandah, was one of the emotional highlights in the film. (Paradoxically, she was to give a bold Freudian interpretation to her Ophelia in Gielgud's *Hamlet* which she did on the stage in 1936. The frenzied sexual writhing on the floor reminded those who had seen it of the subconscious and profoundly sensual manner in which, in Griffith's *Birth of a Nation*, after a particular bout of girlish leaping about and clapping of hands, the way Griffith's heroines were wont to do, she suddenly fell against a bed post and clasped it to her breast with startling passion.)

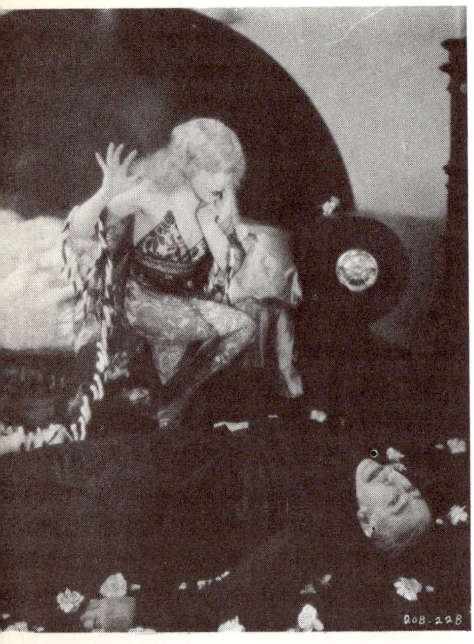

MAE MURRAY
Mae Murray of the bee-stung lips and dreaming eyes, as Kitty O'Hara who becomes *The Merry Widow*.

The Merry Widow.
Idol of Clay.

Lillian Gish earned the devotion of two of the geniuses of her time, Griffith and Max Reinhardt, and one of its wits, George Jean Nathan, but gained as well, the subtle and persistent enmity of the powerful Photoplay magazine, which, according to the actress Louise Brooks, was doing M.G.M.'s hatchet job for them. Whether or not this is true, despite her stage training which should have opened up a whole new career for her when the talkies came, her career as one of the movies' greatest stars was effectively finished with her M.G.M. contract. In later years she returned as a much-sought-after character actress, but never again as the heroine.

The 30s were in truth more romantic because of the air of reality that had swept into the film studios. Audiences had grown a little more mature with the loss of their livelihood and now demanded films and stories that seemed more realistic than before. Poverty is a great maturing agent. But the 20s was a hot-house all to itself. The movies in that era and the brightest luminaries were like the expatriates from one of Huysmans's fruitier novels. The ladies Swanson and Negri, domestic and foreign allurers, wreckers of homes and quickeners of pulses, fought for supremacy in studio and on screen, but had the saving grace to see the inherent ridiculousness in the situation. They were both Queen Bees, each with their own hives; Pola's in Hollywood and Swanson's at the Astoria Studios in New York. Between and below them came other aspirants, the Naldis and Pringles, the Godowskys and the Goudals, and the ravishing Barbara La Marr, whom they called too beautiful to live. (Years later when M.G.M. brought Hedy Kiesler to Hollywood and changed her name to suit her image, they recalled the other mistress of dark shadows, and Hedy Lamarr was born.) There were a legion of others who vamped up a storm in the films they appeared in. But one of the greatest and most self-enchanted of that enchanting lot, was Mae Murray, who straddled dreamy heights of make-believe that stars would never again be able to reach.

Mae Murray, undeniably one of the most popular stars of the era, usually gets short-shrift from today's historians in much the same way that she got it from the critics in her time, who seemed nettled to find that the public did not take their send-ups and put-downs of her screen frolics seriously. For the public adored her no matter how acidly the reviews read. They went to her movies with disbelief securely kept out and accepted her wildly improbable plots and behaviour, her bizarre coiffures and the mad clothes that were designed to show off her small but lily-white body. Bizarre in behaviour and dress and longings, she fulfilled all the little-girl fantasies to dress up in fancy clothes and go to the ball. True, Gloria Swanson's early starring films, especially those she made for Cecil B. De Mille, were only a little less improbable, but Swanson had a marvellous sense of comedy, and as her star rose and she had the power to select her own scripts, her films became better, and funnier.

Mae's naïveté was eye-popping even for the period (at any rate to the critics). But, while mothers railed against her in the columns of the fan magazines, for her daring poses and provocative dances (only a 20s mother, having been a Victorian child, could have taken her seriously as a threat to the morals of her offspring), the teenagers of the day madly aped her clothes and look, and the girls covered up their mouth and most of their faces when painting on the 'bee stung' lips Mae had. Her mouth alone was a three-ring circus affair and certainly would not have been as innocent on anyone else. The implication was blatant, but her behaviour was too improbable so the one cancelled out the other.

But it was Mae Murray's films that helped to tide M.G.M. over until they got established. Her films were summed up by one reproachful fan who said 'Mae Murray seems to think of all the things a girl would not do in real life and then does them'. One of her husbands, Robert Z. Leonard, directed her in most of her films but after their divorce, others tried with varying degrees of success. Josef von Sternberg, then beginning, started to work on *The Masked Bride* ('25) but after a few days' shooting turned the camera to the ceiling and walked off the set. Erich von Stroheim went on to direct her in one of his best and her most famous films, *The Merry Widow*. John Gilbert was her co-star, but it was a Mae Murray film in a von Stroheim setting. Its immortality was pre-ordained.

Mae Murray played little Kitty O'Hara, stranded American showgirl in some Balkan kingdom, where swine came in two varieties: the four-footed trotters and the mustachio-twirling kind. Old Ruritania was full of the latter or so it seemed from the stories told by Hollywood's authority in these matters, the English authoress, Elinor Glyn. Enter dashing Prince Danilo, trim of moustache, keen of eye and bold of hand; it was always Stroheim's way to break with tradition, and for a time the hero does not behave much better than the villain. Kitty, after a lot of disappointments, marries an incredibly rich and even more incredibly kinky old Baron, whose fetishism for ladies' feet and footwear is so acute that he drops dead on their wedding night at the sight of her bare toes. Still pure, widowed and rich she now looks to drown her sorrows by going to big parties where she would be the centre of attention. She runs into Prince Danilo in time for the Merry Widow Waltz – this is where Franz Lehar briefly comes into the story. The villainous Crown Prince and Danilo fight a duel over the Widow's hand. Danilo is wounded but Kitty, sure now of his love, tends him back to health under the largest bough of apple blossoms any never-never land ever saw. Because of von Stroheim's brilliant direction, Mae Murray had her finest hour in *The Merry Widow*. Few of her films could properly be called romantic, even when they were meant to be. But what she lacked in style she more than made up for in magic.

Paralleling Mae Murray's career was that of Pola Negri – the two lives even overlapping when Mae married Prince Mdvani, and Pola married his brother. Pola Negri has always said, and others agree, that she arrived in Hollywood ahead of her time. In any case, she had a highly colourful career based on her rich romantic Slav personality. Her reputation as an actress was established in her silent German films, and was confirmed by the six German films she made in the mid-30s when Hollywood decided to dispense with her talents. Her low, resonant voice added fresh fascination – a dip in its velvet tones conveyed experiences which contemporary morality could only hint at by a caption reading. 'Pola was that rare hybrid, a good actress as well as a great personality – both of which were made for films. She was at her best when those qualities were united, but she ran better than most on only one of her engines.' When she first arrived in Hollywood, the reaction was mixed. 'Her fellow actresses treated her like a tax collector calling for additional money, while she treated them like something the janitor forgot to sweep up', wrote an anonymous chronicler of the day.

POLA NEGRI
With Conway Tearle in *Bella Donna* (1923).

Born in Poland, of ancestry and date forever confused (with her help), Pola Negri arrived in Hollywood in 1922, already the most popular star both in Europe and in America, where her films were among the first German films to be shown since the end of the war. Conflicting stories circulated about her before she ever arrived. She had a reputation as the greatest emotional actress of the day. Her realistic and highly effective display of high-powered love-making in German films like *Carmen*, *Passion* (*Du Barry*) and *Sumurun* – directed by the best director she ever had, Ernst Lubitsch – and, as important to her female public, her European clothes-sense, her collection of jewels, *and* her title from a dissolved marriage to the Polish Count Dambski, were God-given material for the publicity machines that Paramount set up. Here was real gold where they were used to costume jewellery! Charlie Chaplin, then already the 'Idol' of the world, had met her in Berlin a year earlier and had come back raving about 'the greatest emotional actress and woman in Europe'. Their much-publicized affair (about which both provided quite different slants in their eventual autobiographies) only helped to fan local rivalries and national expectations. In the event, her first American film, *Bella Donna*, and most of the follow-ups were considered decidedly disappointing by both the worked-up public and the worshipful critics, who had done their share to praise her in advance. The blame was squarely laid on Hollywood's shoulders in trying to turn a mountain cat into a household pet. Her three-dimensional and highly emotive personality in wildly improbable two-dimensional characters could not help but overburden them. The diminishing effect of this on her popularity would not tell immediately, and there followed *Forbidden Paradise* (her only American film with Lubitsch,

whose analytical, satirical approach meshed well with her instinctive, emotional one). Their films together made both their reputations, and both were crowned in Hollywood. *Hotel Imperial* and *Barbed Wire* were also personal and artistic triumphs – though coming too late, when it was virtually impossible to revive the slump in her personal pull.

Typical of her usual material were such efforts as *Crown of Lies, Men, Three Sinners* and *The Woman from Moscow*, in which she always played world-weary women in situations which common sense would have told her to walk out of long before. In *The Woman from Moscow*, Pola '. . . took the oath! She swore she would find the man who had slain her fiancé. She swore to avenge his death. She found the man. But she discovered she could not go through with her threat. Life held a new terror for her now!' The film was typical of what Paramount thought suitable for Pola.

The Crown of Lies was . . . 'A story of charm and power with Pola Negri throughout ready to sacrifice herself for the happiness of others. The leading man is a gum-chewing, go-getting, typical automobile salesman. It has, moreover, a big epic note based on faith. The myth of a queen who can perform miracles becomes a reality, in that miracles begin to happen of their own accord.' It required a miracle to make the film work, and none was forthcoming.

In *Men* she was a famous dancer in Paris, once wronged by one of the breed and ever since paying the lot of them back by pouring glasses of water over them in fits of pent-up anger. 'Men go nightly to see her on stage and throw their hearts and fortunes at her feet, but she picks up only the money, which she gives to girls who struggle as she has struggled.'

A lighter actress could have made more out of wildly improbable subjects like those and *The Cheat, Shadows of Paris* or *Bella Donna*. Mae Murray had of course done just that, but Negri's realistic approach knocked the already threadbare stories out of joint.

A welcome change of pace for her was director Mal St Clair's light and amused handling of *Woman of The World* ('23). It was poles apart from her other films insofar as she was charming, amusing and modern and played a Polish countess stranded in a mid-Western American town, a situation allowing many digs and references to American small-town puritanism and inverted snobbery.

Frustration with her roles meant that she began to overact, on screen and, it seemed, in life. The beginning of her end came with Valentino's death. As tempestuous lovers, both their careers had been given a colourful new impetus after his divorce from his wife. Valentino's death was sudden and unexpected. Her cross-country trip from Los Angeles to New York to get to his funeral, accompanied by her repeated swooning from grief, was mocked cruelly by the press and made her appear more a hysterical than a romantic soul in agony.

A tragedienne can take anything except ridicule – it exposes to a harsh glare the very qualities that seemed so romantic the night before. Up till then, Pola's beautifully dressed but virtually empty vehicles had fooled the public if only by the effort she herself put in. Now, the accumulation of foolish films and exotic behaviour conspired to undermine her American career.

All her films had superb production values; the finest technical and photographic work expended on them, but the romantic star requires more than a director's props to keep the illusion alive. So, Pola, whom her studio had glowingly heralded as 'mistress of moods, lady of love, radiant regent of romance', abdicated and returned to Europe for a spell just as the talkies came in.

Her roles had been a far cry from the fiery, sexy and humorous heroines of her German films. Hollywood, by changing the fiery gypsy into a thinner, more glamorous, more beautiful woman to conform to popular taste, removed the spark. But she had been the first great foreign star to come to Hollywood and equal her triumph abroad.

THE ARCHITECTURAL SPLENDOUR OF GLORIA SWANSON

Don't Change Your Husband **(1918).** *For Better For Worse.*

Pola's rival at Paramount was Gloria Swanson. Gloria had risen via Cecil B. De Mille's sexy tales of moral retribution and high jinks, from the ranks of Mack Sennett comedies to the position of clothes-horse de luxe, the far out young modern of the day, daring, permissive – though a good girl at heart. By 1925 she was Paramount's biggest money-making star. She was reported to be the second woman to have earned a million dollars and the first to spend it, some of it on her five husbands. She was quoted years after as saying her tombstone should read 'I paid the bills'. When she left Paramount in 1926 to go into production on her own and joined the independents at United Artists, Zukor offered her a million dollars a year to stay with them. She stuck out for total autonomy at U-A instead.

American born, brought up with a shrewd awareness of what the American public expected of her and what she could do best, Gloria Swanson triumphed while Pola succumbed. Like Pola and Mae and Mary Pickford for that matter, Swanson was not very tall (few of the imperious sirens were). She had a genuine and very active sense of humour which carried over into her films as well as being a varied and intelligent actress. She controlled her career and anticipated the public's change of interests in much the same way that she designed and redesigned herself to make the most of her good points. De Mille having shown her the power of clothes, she developed a fashion flair and brought Paris to Indiana. Her face was architectural in its contours, the size of the head, the ski-slope nose, the wide-apart and glowing eyes, the determined chin, gave her an unique ability to vary her roles from haughty demeanour to knockabout comedy (as in the delightful subway scenes in *Manhandled*) with equal facility and conviction. A critic once wrote that Swanson's greatest achievement was her face in repose. In films like *Stage Struck* in which she played a hash-house waitress with ambitions that were only realized in dream-sequences she showed an ability to get herself into ridiculous scrapes without detracting from her appeal. This allowed for hilarious accidents like a flea circus that escapes and finds a new berth on her (in *Fine Manners*).

Swanson blended glamour and screwball comedy that would serve later stars like Carole Lombard and Lucille Ball. Her roles were so varied, her use of her talents so shrewd that no one film properly sums up her qualities, though most of them contained what audiences expected of her. Again, the romance was more in her personality than

Joan Crawford – A star for all seasons.

Hedy Lamarr, the fairest of them all.

in the stories – though she made specifically romantic films like *Coast of Folly*, in which she played three generations of women – mother, daughter and granddaughter, a tour de force for her as an actress. The publicity for her films gives only a scarce hint at the quality in the films themselves and that in terms of expense, but they do help to convey the general aura of frolic and folly that marked the era.

The titles for her films with De Mille, which did so much to project her to the public as the 'American sophisticate', tell their own stories: *Don't Change Your Husband* ('19) (which brought her with her peacock-feathered headdress into the white-hot light of publicity: she became the rage; she was imitated wherever films were shown. Keepers of aviaries looked suspiciously at any young modern passing the birdcages after a number of the more exotic species were found denuded overnight), *For Better For Worse, Male and Female, Why Change Your Wife* ('20), *Something To Think About, The Affairs of Anatole* ('21), all wagged an admonishing finger in the last reel at the goings-on depicted in the preceding ones. In them, De Mille used her mostly for her knack of wearing clothes that would be copied by shopgirls and laughed at by the fashionable. Her reputation as a clothes-horse was continued without let-up in her subsequent starring films. Much was made of her wardrobe in the publicity for films like *Beyond The Rocks* ('21). Teaming her with Rudolph Valentino the publicity read 'Come and see this great new drama by the authoress of *Three Weeks*. See the beautiful star of *The Great Moment* and *Her Husband's Trademark* and her fifty luxurious new gowns.' *Her Husband's Trademark* promised 'Glorious Gloria in a super-spectacular picture story of throbbing romance, adventurous thrills and luxurious beauty. She wears, as the best-dressed woman in New York, forty gorgeous gown creations, the last word in fashion.'

Swanson came of extremely mixed stock – Polish-French-German extraction on her mother's side, and Swedish and Italian on her father's, the fusion of which no doubt helped her to be the sort of American who could well understand the tastes of Americans everywhere by relying on her own. Like Joan Crawford and Lana Turner, Swanson built up her career by understanding better than her producers what her public wanted.

Compared to the headiness of the exotic sirens and women of the world, Norma Talmadge was apple pie dressed up in cream and fancy trappings. Her speciality was the woman's weepies. She was not as beautiful as Corinne Griffiths nor as fine an emotional actress as Pauline Frederick, but she possessed the quality women identified with to a greater extent than either. She began her screen career as early as 1910 and was already noticed as the pathetic little milliner in a production of *A Tale of Two Cities* (1911), opposite matinée idol Maurice Costello. Such was the then power of the moving image on spectators that a very short moment on the screen made audiences notice. By 1920, Talmadge had become the most fashionable woman in the United States. Everything she wore, since her clothes had a breath of reality amidst all the make-believe glad-rags the others wore, was copied by her legions of admirers. By now also she had become the specialist in the sort of romantic heroines Norma Shearer

Hedy Lamarr, the fairest of them all.

Sadie Thompson **(1928).**
Queen Kelly **(1928).**

Swanson's Norma Desmond (*Sunset Boulevard*: 1950), whose extravagant grandeur, for all its desperation, was a staggering testimonial to a time that would be no more.

would take over with equal success in the 30s, Greer Garson in the 40s and Grace Kelly in the 50s. The audience thought them to be what was meant by a woman who was called a lady – by quality rather than by birth.

Norma Talmadge's great romantic successes were *Secrets, Smilin' Through, Camille, Ashes Of Vengeance* and similar works. *Secrets* and *Smilin' Through* (discussed elsewhere) were among the most popular films of the era. Both were re-made with enormous success in sound, though not with her. By 1931, after the abysmal failure of the second talkie, *Du Barry*, she retired from films. For most of her career she specialized shrewdly in sob and smile roles like those mentioned earlier; the woman who gave and paid. Clarence Brown, who directed her in *Kiki*, one of her few returns to comedy, thought she was one of the best comediennes he had ever worked with, but her fans would have none of it. Humour, anything more than a gentle long-suffering smile, was out of the question. To her public she was always a lady, whether she appeared as a native dancing-girl, shop-lifter or even a whore. The reverse was true of her sister, Constance, a very popular comedienne in sophisticated roles.

One of Norma's early films, *Panthea* (1917), established her in the type of roles she would have her great vogue in. Those of a brave and tragic and self-sacrificing heroine in beautiful clothes who sheds tears amid opulent surroundings and finds redemption just before the fade-out. Besides her own attractive and restrained acting style, she made sure of the screen-plays by having two of the best women writers of the day, Anita Loos and Frances Marion, write most of her films. Miss Marion, who wrote virtually all of Norma's 1917–27 films, had done the same for Mary Pickford, would do it for Valentino (*The Eagle* and *Son of The Sheik*) and later, for Garbo, Marie Dressler and others. Hers was a great talent, all the more valuable for having grown up in films, understanding the demands and limitations the medium set and imposed, and possessing a sensitive but clear-eyed shrewdness allied to an artistic nature. Miss Marion's scripts were able to tear off the dross and whip up a freshness that managed to balance the film in favour of intelligence, characterization and believability. She was one of the finest of the creative writers to come from the movies. Miss Loos, a clever young woman who wrote many of Douglas Fairbanks's early comedies, went on to write *Gentlemen Prefer Blondes*, which did a lot to change public tastes in the women men love but don't marry, from fatal brunettes to peroxided blondes.

NORMA TALMADGE
The Song of Love **(1924).**

Talmadge's only serious rival was Corinne Griffiths, whose fairy-tale beauty as Emma Hamilton in *The Divine Lady* **(1929) seemed to step out of a Romney portrait.**

Norma's father was a Jewish travelling salesman and her mother was Irish, the classic American mixture. She had the romantic dark colouring of her father's race, and her mother's tenacity and shrewdness. One of the classic 'stage mothers', she also propelled her other two daughters into film careers. By the time the talkies arrived Norma had been a star for twenty years and her career was on the wane. The two talkies she made cut it short. 'Time' wrote: 'In her first dialog effort (*New York Nights* ('29)) she talked like an elocution pupil. This time (*Du Barry – Woman Of Passion* ('30)) she talks like an elocution teacher!' Anyway, Norma Shearer was beginning to rise in the public's affection to the same heights in similar if more modernized roles. The equally shrewd and attractive Miss Shearer, having done what Norma Talmadge had done early in her career and married a producer, was guided by Irving Thalberg from then on. The public could continue to see the same films they had loved the old Norma in, starring a new and younger Norma. To make the transfer complete, Norma Talmadge dropped out of the public sight – a very rich woman for the rest of her private life. The 20s were rounded off as it were by the arrival on the scene half-way through the decade of two epoch-making stars of the screen, Garbo and Clara Bow. But before going into their careers I would like to digress and point out two other signal dark lodestars who could not be properly typed, but once seen would prove unforgettable: Louise Brooks and Evelyn Brent.

LOUISE BROOKS

The Canary Murder Case **(1929).**

Brooks had Pabst, Brent had von Sternberg. Both directors saw to it that they achieved lasting fame, having survived poor vehicles by lesser directors. They were almost perfect opposites, which makes it almost irresistible to pair them off here. Brooks had a round face, a pert mouth, black bands of straight dark hair, and a figure that was boyish above the waist and decidedly feminine elsewhere. She moved like a dancer, which in fact she had been and would be again after her career was finished. Brent, on the other hand, was angular and hollow-cheeked and sombre in disposition. Together they appeared in one feature, *Love 'Em And Leave 'Em* ('26), which Louise stole without much effort, having the better role – that of the amoral but engaging younger sister to Brent's no-nonsense, straight-from-the-shoulder heroine.

Brooks was overtly erotic, Brent a femme fatale, although more fatale to herself than to the men in her life. Like Barbara Stanwyck, who brought a neurotic edge to the same type of roles, Brent paid her dues and owed the world nothing. Happy endings were not her thing. In *Underworld*, her first picture with von Sternberg, she played Feathers McCoy, hard as nails and soft as feathers. She is, however, redeemed by her reluctant admiration for a sodden ex-lawyer (Clive Brook), and she is suspected of the worst by her protector, Bull (George Bancroft). Brent was the perfect moll, a part she was to play over and over, as in *The Dragnet*, her last film with von Sternberg. Between these two films, she also appeared with Emil Jannings in von Sternberg's Russian drama, *The Last Command*, as a revolutionary whose fate is sealed when she allows a Czarist General to escape, a role that anticipates those of the Dietrichs to come. The last image of her in the film, as she leans far out from the train as it pitches into the dark, had all the imagistic power of Dietrich facing the shooting squad in *Dishonoured*. Sound gave her a voice to match her quality, and even uninspired direction in countless B-films which followed could not diminish it.

Brooks had been in a Broadway chorus when she was signed by Paramount to make her first movie, *American Venus* ('25). Flat chested but far from boyish, it seemed as if her youth and looks would doom her to a career as a second-string Colleen Moore. But she began to be noticed in films like *A Girl In Every Port* ('27) as the last but most memorable of the girls two American sailors love and leave only to fall out with each other over her, and *Beggars Of Life*, where she masqueraded as a boy to escape being noticed by her fellow hobos while on the road. The German director G. W. Pabst saw her in one of her films, imported her to Berlin and built two films around her, *Pandora's Box* ('28) and *Diary of a Lost Girl* ('29). Out of the latter he fashioned a definitive version of Lulu, the reckless, laughing and amoral heroine of Wedekind's plays. (Asta Nielsen and Nadja Tiller essayed the role before and after Brooks, but none compared with the Lulu Pabst created.) Overnight, she was the darling of European intelligentsia. And time proved that she was infinitely more aware and perceptive than her contemporaries: in her memoirs, hopefully to be published some day, Brooks casts a baleful eye on the film industry of her time, dissecting a few choice specimens with unusual candour and insight.

Brooks was never more appealing, however, than in her one French film, *Prix De Beauté*, from a story by René Clair and directed by Auguste Genina, which anticipated *La Signora De Tutti* and even *Sunset Boulevard*, although this time, the Girl with the Face also had a few words (even if they were dubbed in by a French actress). The heroine of *Prix De Beauté* does not live to be forgotten by her public like Norma Desmond, but dies on the screening-room floor, shot by her neglected working-class husband, while her glorious face, forever preserved on celluloid, sings from the screen the film's haunting refrain: 'Don't be jealous of me, I have but one love, and it's you.' Brooks seemed as sexually liberated on the screen as the recent Maria Schneider. She was inquisitive, and never backed out of a new experience. In *Pandora's Box*, she dances with a Lesbian at her wedding, and ends in the arms of Jack the Ripper, a look of orgasmic pleasure on her face. In *Diary of A Lost Girl*, she was the happy inmate of a whorehouse. Circumstances put her there, but the *joie de vivre* with which she accepted her fate was strictly her own.

EVELYN BRENT
Last Command **(1928).**
Underworld **(1927).**

Brooks faced Death with desire still on her eyes and mouth. Brent came to it with a sense of peace denied her in life. Both were fortunate enough to find a genius who saw through the conventions of make-up and typecasting, and brought out their very unique qualities.

Diametrically opposed to any of the romantic heroines so far mentioned and especially the soulful Garbo was Clara Bow, the 'IT' Girl and the personification of all the fun and fad consciousness of the era that had embraced so many diverse types in its affection, and of its fall from grace.

In the midst of Clara's madcap scrapes one sensed, saw revealed, in sudden moving glimpses, an emotional creature of great depth and feelings. She was a life force – restless, moving, looking forward to the next man, the next movie, the next experience. Not that Clara attempted to communicate a psychological complex character in her films. On the contrary, her loquacious forthright manner was one of her most appealing assets. Forty years later, her films could be shown to an international audience of critics and journalists in a retrospective of American silent films where again, undiminished by time, her radiance filled the cinema. To a man and a woman, they poured out,

searching for adjectives to describe her, and settling for the one Elinor Glyn had once coined and which stuck. Clara was 'IT'. Like Marilyn Monroe years later, she was a capable and charming actress and comedienne, and she could if necessary rise to high drama. 'Beautiful, restless, aggressively young and alive, Clara Bow *was* the twenties' wrote David Robinson.

Clara Bow was born in Brooklyn (home as well of Mae West, Susan Hayward, Barbara Stanwyck, Veronica Lake and others) of French, Scottish and English descent and raised in extreme poverty. She entered films by winning the 'Fame and Fortune' contest advertised in the film magazines. She was only fifteen when she made her first film *Beyond The Rainbow* in 1922 but the part hit the cutting-room floor. As a refuge from her grim life she spent most of her time going to the movies. Once she had a foot in the door she worked hard and persevered. She gained attention when she was hired for the secondary role in the whaling drama, *Down To The Sea In Ships* ('23) and began to move up from then on. The public had begun to single her out. She was given a small role by Ernst Lubitsch in *The Marriage Circle*. She made fourteen films in 1925, eight in 1926 and six in 1927. It was a gruelling pace but her popularity with the public, who could not get enough of her, made her the most popular star in films. The film *It* based on the Elinor Glyn novelette consolidated her position. Miss Glyn when asked who had IT, replied that besides Clara, her doorman and *Rin-Tin-Tin* also possessed the mysterious quality. Better than anyone, she mirrored the American modern of the day – the girls behind shop-counters, manicurists, stenographers and secretaries. When Pola Negri left Paramount, Clara was given her dressing room, then the largest and greatest status-symbol. She was the flapper par excellence, and jazzed up programmes like *The Plastic Age* ('25) and others. Her films were as far-fetched (though strictly modern) as any, but Clara was not. She was real. Most of the parts she was given – *Rough House Rosie, Three Weekends, Get Your Man* – had to be carried by her personality, but there were some that revealed the range she would have grown into if she had not retired so early.

CLARA BOW
In a sophisticated moment.

Victor Fleming directing Clara Bow, Percy Marmont as the lawyer and Ernest Torrence as her doting husband in *Mantrap*.

Perhaps the first film to do more than hint at Clara's full scope and which even now remains one of the most charming of her films was *Mantrap* ('26) directed with unmistakable fondness for the young actress by the older and sophisticated Victor Fleming who also directed her in *Hula* ('27). As a cuticle-pusher in the big city, Clara meets a rough but good-hearted hick from the backwoods who offers her a home of her own. When her husband brings back a lawyer friend from the city on his annual hunting trip, she feels attracted to his civilized manners and charm. He reciprocates, responding to her playful sensuality and loveliness. The two agree to run away but the trip downriver brings her back to her senses. She realizes that beside her providing husband, he is ineffectual and unable to cope with the realities of life in the wild as they arise (tin cans and no opener in the food supply he packed). When her husband catches up with them, concerned only to make sure that she is happy, she knows where her happiness lies. It was an unqualified hit and pushed her into stardom, much against her will at the time. The film was outstanding for its very beautiful, near-erotic moments. One such came when the two fleeing lovers rest on a river bank at night. Clara, slightly mussed from paddling and coping with the setting up of the camp, responds to his romancing as they sit by the fire. Her head is tilted back, her eyes are open, their glance is unashamed. The soft brown hair blowing away from her forehead reveals a near-naked face of a vibrant carnality.

GARBO – evolving from the temptress to Ninotchka.

At the peak of her success, little scandals involving the alienation of the affections of other girls' husbands only added to her fascination. A gambling scandal – she had foolishly written IOUs for more money than she carried with her – did her less good. But the worst check to her career was when she charged her secretary Daisy De Vee with embezzlement; and the affronted Daisy countered in court with talk of drink and drugs and worse. The daily revelations, which had nothing to do with the case, turned the trial into a three-ring circus, while Clara's life made the headlines. The emotional set-backs she received then were to affect her in later life.

But the legend that her voice was not good enough for the talkies was nonsense. Her few talking films reveal just the sort of voice you would expect – bright, brittle, and with just a touch of Brooklyn which sounded best when she was putting on the Ritz. In her first talkie, *The Wild Party*, she was still the old Clara, playing the madcap at a girls' college who sets her sights at the handsome new anthropology tutor (Fredric March), and managing, as always, to get into a good deal of trouble and undress.

In the films of her brief comeback ('32–'33) she is still irresistible, but more mature; the figure fuller and even more seductive, the face rounder, the voice a little deeper. In *Call Her Savage* her Thirties-model gowns cling to her in a way far more revealing than nudity. She had a miraculously sensuous way of adjusting a shoulder strap or tucking her blouse into the belt of her skirt, having dislodged it while horse-whipping the man she really loves for an unprovoked impertinence. *Call Her Savage* was Clara Bow's *Blonde Venus* – a tale of mother-love without Dietrich's fatalism. Clara, having no such controlling force as Dietrich's von Sternberg, takes the movie into her capable hands and storms into marriage, motherhood, sacrifice and redemption. She was modern woman taking fate into her own hands and moving right on. One of her strongest weapons was her beauty and sexuality which she used unskimpingly. 'Not a little of her sex-appeal,' as David Robinson wrote seeing her in the film, 'lies in her impregnability. A fellow who gets too fresh or dares pinch her bottom will end up laid low with a straight right to the jaw. This mixture of sex kitten and militant virgin is peculiarly potent.'

Clara's last days were clouded. She made no films after 1933. Having proved to herself that the public had forgiven her and were more than ready to welcome her back, she felt no further need to carry on. Her marriage to Rex Bell, the cowboy star and sometime governor of Nevada, broke up, though they never divorced. The restlessness and vitality that were her charm came to torment her; she was a chronic insomniac and spent much of the later years in and out of sanatoriums. She died alone, sitting up in bed watching television, in 1965.

Greta Garbo's appeal was clearly to both sexes and to all generations, and yet belonged to no type before her. It was not so much that she went against any established conventions (her films made sure of that) but that she herself was outside of the conventional. She was erotic, mysterious and solitary. She dominated situations and co-stars with a masculine vigour, but became sublimely feminine in solitude, with nature, animals and children.

Garbo was the screen's greatest romantic star, as much a fictional heroine as those she played so perfectly. To men she was the pagan, to women the spiritual side of the female symbol – the woman who at one and the same time was the downfall of Adam and the mother of God. Garbo's silence off the screen might have been genuinely inspired, but was more probably a very shrewd touch, the result of her self-consciousness. The studios' acquiescence when they realized that a remote Garbo was better publicity than an inarticulate one was hardly surprising. The early interviews she gave shed light on the person but not on the enigma. Writers had more fun speculating than reporting. Garbo, a young, unsure, twenty-year-old, was sensitive to being described as a village-oaf for her awkward movements off the camera or as 'a stupid, lovely fool' because she had difficulty answering questions in English when her eloquence on film spoke across nations. Too much of that sort of exposure could have damaged her (there was Pola Negri's career to warn) and the studio knew this. In the face of her silence, writers for fan magazines, sophisticated glossies and even the highbrow monthlies, came under the spell of her image, writing about her as if she were a character out of the realms of romantic fiction. Articles and reviews seemed to describe the further adventures of a Georges Sand heroine. There is an historical rather than revealing interest in quoting one of her early interviews, to show the disparity between reality and myth, the sort of instant mythmaking processing that the movies were so adept at creating, though never to the same degree as with Garbo.

After the release of her first American film, *The Torrent* (her Swedish and German films were only shown in America after she had become established), the demand for features about and interviews with her was at a feverish pitch. No-one, least of all the studio, could have foreseen the sensation this decidedly modest story from one of Ibanez's books would create. It is about a woman who is doomed never to have the man she loves while the world throws its fortunes at her feet. Garbo had thought it bad while making it, though it was not much worse than similar vehicles usually given to foreigners.

A woman reporter for 'Motion Picture' on the set watching her at work (she was then making *The Temptress* as a follow-up to cash in on the interest – again a story by Ibanez – again as a sexy temptress who leaves men in her wake like a hurricane) wrote:

'When you speak with her, it is impossible to fathom whether she's the subtlest, most highly intelligent woman on earth, or the stupidest loveliest fool. She is reserved. She lets you talk while she sighs and smokes.

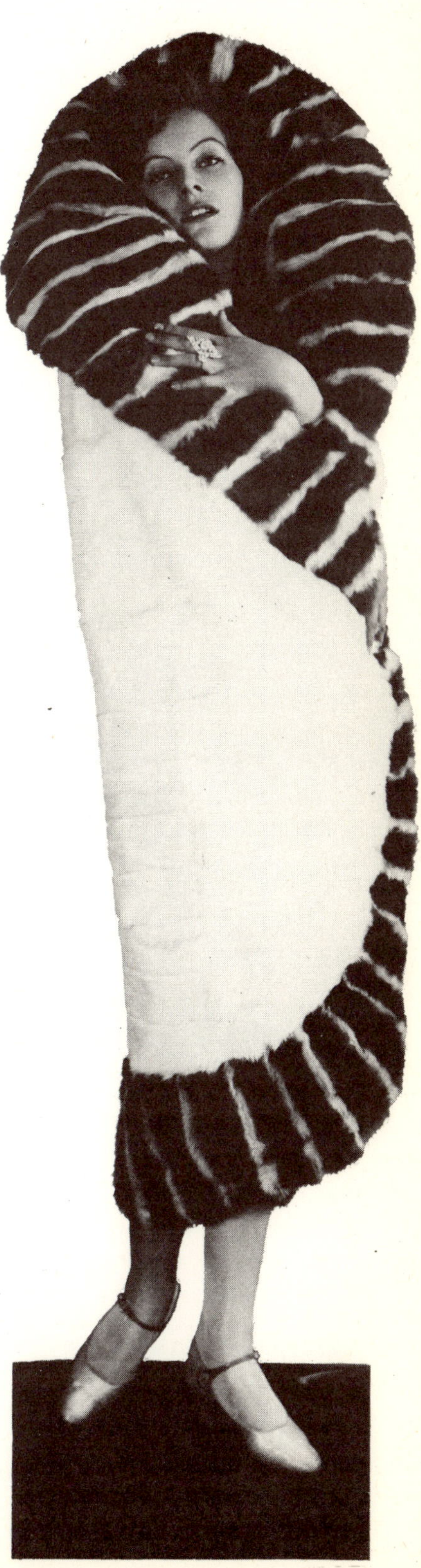

"What do you do for amusement when your work is done?" I asked.
"No-thing."
"Don't you play golf?"
"No-ah."
"Tennis?"
"No-ah."
"Bridge?"
"No-ah."
"Swim, dance, ride, drive or drink?"
"Oh. No-ah."
"Well," exasperated, "what do you do?"
"No-thing. Only wurrk."
And I found it to be true.'
Her work spoke for her.

If it was Garbo's decision to stop giving interviews when she was in a position to do so, it is unlikely – judging from the frustrating ones she gave – that the studio was against it. And once Garbo stopped talking it was easier for all concerned to write about what they thought she might have said.

Garbo's myth was founded on things she did not do, but others thought she did, and those she did do but did not comment on. Garbo was proof positive that silence in private was indeed golden in public.

In later years, when the shadow of another international conflict temporarily swept aside the mysteries and enigmas, it was too late for Garbo to alter her image, had she wanted to again. Her last film was not successful enough for either her or her studio to want to try. Her box-office was slipping. There were more immediate needs, less demanding new stars were rising, and nobody cared enough at the time. So she left in person while the image remained, elevated by her departure which was as clean and direct as any of her other actions and thus infinitely more mysterious because she did it.

B 1952

TEAMS

There was nothing like the screen for bringing people together, whether Astaire and Rogers swirling their way through the penthouses of the 30s, or Macdonald and Eddy declaring at the top of their lungs their undying love for each other through the Ruritanias of romance.

Francis X. Bushman and Beverley Bayne: the screen's great sweethearts until the public discovered they were married in real life. Suddenly romance vanished.

The perfect couple on the screen, Myrna Loy and William Powell, were married to different mates off-screen, but unlike many of the public's favourites, they were good friends.

Piper Laurie and Tony Curtis were a wan imitation of the sort of teams that raced hearts.

The real-life couple, Taylor and Burton, whose passion on film is decidedly flat, in *Cleopatra* (1963).

PART 3: THE TALKIE STARS

The talkies put the melo into the drama. The human voice added the dimension that was missing, for the star if not for the medium. Whatever sound may have done to the art of the film, it did wonders for the sagas of struggle, sacrifice and redemption which were the prerogative of stars. To accommodate the demands of sound a new school of acting and a new wave of faces swept across world cinema, eclipsing many of the legends of the preceding decade as if they were memories from the dark ages.

Some, of course, made the transition: Garbo's voice was to confirm the legend of her personality. In silent films, the muted eloquence of her gestures, the deep unspoken mysteries in her eyes, had been the pantomime of a great artist who could forever be undermined by the inadequate captions of a title-writer. Now, with her voice, she could transfigure banalities as easily as she soared to dramatic heights, for sound gave to her what it perversely took from so many others: there was a landscape to her voice as there was in her face.

What Garbo transcended by her art, Bette Davis blew sky-high with hers. But Joan Crawford, by believing that what she played on the screen was true and offering her own life as evidence, enveloped herself in the American Dream. The story of her life, her struggle to become 'the greatest star of them all', is ideal material for films like those she built her name on. Awe-inspiring Joan Crawford! Her strong-jawed, superb face lit up by hypnotic large eyes, ambition burning fiercely in that intense mien and defiance squaring her already broad shoulders as she blazed through the five-and-ten Cinderella stories in which she specialized.

JOAN CRAWFORD
Sadie McKee.
The Bride Wore Red **(1937).**
La Suprema surrounded by men in her first appearance as the self-destructive, rich society beauty who discovers and falls for a talented violinist from the other side of the tracks. Crawford was superb in a performance that harked back to the romantic agonizing of the Italian divas for its effect in this wild and wonderful dramatization of *Humoresque* **(1946).**
The Damned Don't Cry

Sadie McKee ('34) was the prototype of the roles Joan Crawford played in the 30s. Sadie McKee, the cook's daughter on a big estate, grows up as playmate to the son of the house, David (played by Franchot Tone, her husband as well as her co-star at the time – both of which supporting roles he soon abandoned). Sadie falls in love with a boy from her own side of the tracks, and follows him to the big city where he promptly deserts her. She meets a self-made millionaire, whom she likes but does not love, and agrees to marry him much to the chagrin of David, now grown-up and the tycoon's lawyer and friend. To save her alcoholic husband from himself, she tells the hostile household staff not to interfere with her cure, giving a speech that it is hard to imagine any other actress than Crawford taking so seriously. She doesn't tell the servants. She inspires them.

Set free, and well set up by her grateful and cured husband, Sadie, who had lost track of her one true love, gets detectives to find him; when they do, he is penniless and tubercular. Sadie does the one possible thing: she places him in a sanatorium, where he dies.

At the film's conclusion, David is celebrating his birthday (he has remained a friend throughout). Sadie's mother tells him he will have one wish granted if he blows out the candles with one breath. David looks across the table and gives Crawford a look of silent longing. As he blows the candles out, the room and the screen darken. It is the kind of off-the-cuff poetry the genre constantly surprises one with, and at which Clarence Brown, who directed, was skilled.

Sadie was made several years before Joan Crawford became the Great Emasculator, in films like *Humoresque, Queen Bee, Harriet Craig* and *Mildred Pierce*. But in 30s roles like *Letty Lynton*, Mary Turner in *Paid*, or Borzage's *Mannequin*, she played heroines who had one dream: to move from Hell's Kitchen facing the Hudson River, to a Sutton Place penthouse overlooking the East River. Her few forays into more elevated subjects showed that she was just as good in them. Metro-Goldwyn-Mayer's *Grand Hotel* ('32) was a classic example, with Crawford stealing the film from the most admired actors of the day, the Barrymore Brothers, Garbo and Wallace Beery. If Crawford decided after that to restrict herself to the sort of films her public demanded it is because she had created an infinitely more exciting, and challenging role – herself. Hers was a personality worth projecting and which she knew how to project. Girls who left home to take a job in the Woolworths of the World, were only following in the footsteps of Joan Crawford. In interviews and articles she confided, advised and dictated the rules of success. 'Sophistication was the fruit of experience,' she told her public. 'It is to my advantage that I know cocktail recipes as well as the most elegant ways of lighting a cigarette. It is a mark of your personality, this indefinable mark of your character, that is forged by life itself.' Garbo's legend was ensured by saying nothing. Crawford's by telling everything.

Jean Arthur

Many names crop up while musing about romantic heroines: Barbara Stanwyck who suffered so eloquently the agonies of the doomed; the straight-shooting, red-headed beauty queen, Ann Sheridan; the technically dazzling, aristocratically profiled and soignée Norma Shearer; Irene Dunne who was mischief and delight, sentiment and a shrug-of-the-shoulder; and the lyrically lovely Loretta Young, who has always been underrated as an actress because her poetic beauty typecast her as fragile victim and romantic heroine. The full range of her talent as well as her resourceful beauty was brought into focus in T.V.'s *Loretta Young Show* which ran for over ten years. Contemporary foreign stars also come to mind – like the elfin child-woman from Germany, Elizabeth Bergner; the warm and intelligent Edna Best from England – and one of the most memorable romantic stars, the Russian-born actress of numerous German movies for more than thirty years, Olga Tschechowa. Here was the type of woman Colette caught perfectly in *Cheri* – older, wiser, understanding – a private smile that hints at good memories. Later there came Joan Fontaine and Dorothy McGuire.

Dorothy McGuire had a face that would have been kept off the screen for ever, if it had not been for her talent. She breathed intelligence, and in *A Tree Grows In Brooklyn* she could make a drab housewife more interesting than all the floozies and sophisticated doxies. In *Claudia* ('43) she played a child-wife who is transformed into a throbbingly sexually mature woman. Claudia, a character created by Rose Francken, appeared in magazines, on radio, in book form and in the theatre, where McGuire made it her own to such a degree that there was even a sequel, *Claudia and David*.

Gene Tierney
Leave Her To Heaven.

Rita Hayworth

Joan Fontaine was prettier than McGuire; she bloomed into a fantastic beauty; was a very serviceable actress and excelled as persecuted heroines in the Hitchcock films that made her a star – *Rebecca*, and then *Suspicion* for which she won an Oscar. She went from being very awkward, gangling and flat-chested (*The Women*) to become the dazzling clothes-horse of Paramount in the mid-40s. She had a wider range and better directors than her sister Olivia de Havilland who played similar roles and won *two* Oscars. Away from Hitchcock she became a lady about town with a sense of humour. Since she was British to begin with, with that porcelain beauty one expects from them, she was excellent in *Jane Eyre*, and in Daphne Du Maurier's *Frenchman's Creek* as a voluptuous Restoration chatelaine. After Max Ophuls's *Letter From An Unknown Woman*, arguably her finest film if not her greatest role, she hardened in the 50s into executive women with neurotic problems. But from 1939–48 she was extremely well served by directors, studios – for a change – and vehicles. Actresses used to complain in the mid-40s that all the good parts went to Ingrid Bergman, but Joan Fontaine had no reason to complain.

But my personal choice for the most romantic heroine of the talkies is Margaret Sullavan. Any mention of romance, and Margaret Sullavan's face is the first to come to my mind, as the most magical of memories. The French writer Ado Kyron called her, 'This sad and astonishing girl'. Hers was by no means a perfect face, though the fine delicacy of her irregular features gave her a distinctive beauty. She could be disturbingly honest and made no secret of the fact that she was embarrassed by her first film, *Only Yesterday* ('33), which skyrocketed her to fame. She had already acted on the stage, before Stahl spotted her during the New York run of *Dinner at Eight*, and insisted on her for the role in *Only Yesterday*. While still on the stage Miss Sullavan met, married and divorced (before either entered films) the sympathetic Henry Fonda. When both were successful Hollywood stars they made a delightful romantic teaming in a good zany comedy *The Moon's Our Home* ('36). Off-screen she built up a reputation for being outspoken, temperamental and a perfectionist, which may have been due to her lack of self-confidence, which resolved itself in bouts with her directors. The worst such entanglement took place during the filming of the Ferenc Molnar whimsy *The Good Fairy* ('35), when director William Wyler at last lost his own considerable temper and told her off in front of the entire company. They were married when the film was finished, but divorced after little more than a year. According to an interview she gave, the reason for the fights between them during the filming, was a difference of opinion on how to interpret the character of the young orphanage girl who becomes a cinema usherette and believes what she sees on the screen. After they had settled on this point, they had another blow up – this time over his direction. 'I'm not keen on him as a director at all. For one thing he's too slow. He is one of those painstaking fellows who will spend a whole day to get a scene that lasts about a minute just right.' She added that during the shooting, Wyler fell in love with her and started taking so many close-ups of her that he was taken off the film; though Carl Laemmle put him back on when the reason for his new

FAVOURITES OF THE 40s

Loretta Young and Tyrone Power – the most beautiful couple of all, they made five films in two years.

Joan Fontaine in 1946.

Dorothy McGuire.

attitude was discovered. She concluded with the forthrightness that always distinguished her: 'I don't think husbands should direct their wives in pictures. I love him as a man – but not as a director.'

Most of her directors and co-workers had only praise and affection for her. Borzage directed her in four films; their first and her second film was *Little Man, What Now?* ('34), an American version of the German film from the novel by Hans Fallada, about the struggles of a young couple in pre-Hitler Germany. The other three she made with him at M.G.M. In *Three Comrades* she played the tubercular heroine who sacrifices her life so her husband (Robert Taylor) can have a better future, in a story set again in the Germany of the Depression. *The Shining Hour* ('38) teamed her interestingly with Crawford. The fourth and last film with Borzage was superb – *The Mortal Storm* ('40). Again set in Germany, but this time on the eve of Hitler's rise to power, it showed the effect on one family torn by divided loyalties. This was also her fourth and last teaming with James Stewart who had been a perfect complement to her in *Next Time We Love* ('36), *The Shopworn Angel* ('38) and Ernst Lubitsch's enchanting *The Shop Around The Corner*, one of her best-loved performances.

Sullavan did not exude a conventional glamour that a stills photographer could capture. The best photos of her are snapshots; off-set candids that capture a fraction, a fleeting moment of her incandescent reality. Her honey-husked voice was uniquely sympathetic, but it didn't provide much for star-impersonators, because what gave it that special magic was the thought behind it. It held dreams.

The marvellous thing about her face as in her being was its superb, undiluted, undisguised honesty. The conventional became sublime. Duty, honour, self-sacrifice were moral precepts she conveyed so attractively that they seemed complementary to a witty and original character. Of her, as of very few actresses in my experience, it can be said that she raised the sentimentality inherent in this genre to a creatively true level anyone could admire. For the short time in which she played such types – the clichés disappeared. She lights up her performances with insights into the human character that take the edge off the make-believe without destroying its fragile beauty and appeal. Whatever she played was real – a woman whose frank expression implied 'If I needed to flatter or trick you to win you, by God I don't think I'd want you'.

Only the elusive elfin charms of Jean Arthur were at all comparable to Sullavan. She too could metamorphose the mawkish sentimentality of the parts the studios thought her fit for, and audiences loved her in. Arthur was fortunate in her directors. Frank Capra idolized her, and in their three films gave her roles a resilience and a caustic defensiveness. She was delightfully madcap for directors Mitchel Leisen (*Easy Living*) and George Stevens (*Talk Of The Town* and *The More The Merrier*).

Jean Arthur had been around since 1921, playing leading lady in forgotten programmes for everyone in Hollywood from pie-in-the-face comics to Western heroes. 'The type of girl who isn't supposed to do anything. No-one pays any attention to her,' she said. She had been in movies for more than four years before anyone asked her for an interview. Someone at that period of her life described her as 'oddly controlled for a girl of twenty, her face is childish with young curves and colouring, her eyes are older than the rest of her'. The naturalness that marks her on the screen, that directness in her look, that faith in others that leaves her so exposed and vulnerable, were part of her person from the start. So was the self-defensive shell of cynicism which only made her more appealing, since it never really fooled anyone. 'It took me a long time to get over hoping and believing people's promises. That's the worst of this business. Everyone is such a good promiser. And if a girl lets them get her goat, she's *done.*' And added 'I want a break. I've got to get it before I can quit. If I do get it, perhaps I won't be able to quit.' But she did get it, though much later, and she did quit. The early lack of progress made her decide to go on the stage. Her success in the theatre prompted Hollywood to hire her back, and from 1935 on she was *the* Jean Arthur movie-goers remember and loved. She made a whole series of films with the best directors, from John Ford to Howard Hawks and De Mille, Capra, Billy Wilder and George Stevens. Frank Borzage brought her to the forefront of romantic heroines when she co-starred with Charles Boyer in *History Is Made At Night* ('36). Boyer's restrained passion, his subtle, exploring playing was a perfect complement to her style. The film was a masterpiece.

Even in crinolines, both Sullavan and Arthur were basically modern. But Norma Shearer, first lady of Hollywood in the 30s and

MARGARET SULLAVAN
The Shop Around The Corner **(1940).**

one of the top five box-office stars of the era, was an old-fashioned girl. Shearer was the first lady of Hollywood because she was also the first lady of the screen – that is, she played a lot of ladies! As the wife of one of the most powerful men in Hollywood, Irving Thalberg, she was in a position comparable to that Mary Pickford had in the 20s. She had her choice of the best scripts, but had the intelligence to do those that complemented her own best qualities, and as the ill-fated *Marie Antoinette* ('38) she gave one of the most delicate, low-keyed and intelligent performances of her career. Shearer was not engulfed in the stunningly sumptuous trappings the studio had surrounded her with. The mixture of preciousness and pricelessness which is the charm of Versailles, was her attraction as well. As Marie Antoinette, Norma Shearer was at home. She passed as a sophisticate when the vogue for such roles made it necessary. She wore clothes with great chic and her hairstyles were copied. Where other actresses had eyes, she had a profile. She was adored by her fans as Elizabeth Browning in *The Barretts of Wimpole Street* ('34) and the doomed Moonyean in *Smilin' Through* ('32). Better than any other actress that comes to mind, she fitted the crinolines and hooped skirts of a more graceful era – seeming to step out of rather than into the past, even when, to accommodate the sophistication of the early 30s, she became a lady of drawing-room languour and sophisticated comedies. As *The Divorcée* ('30) she won an Oscar for playing the young modern who goes through many affairs before returning to the husband she always loved best. It was a sign of her professionalism that although she was too spiritual to be convincing in these frivolous and amoral depression dramas – films like *Let Us Be Gay* ('30), *Their Own Desire* ('30), and *Strangers May Kiss* ('31) – she nevertheless could and did have a marked success in them.

NORMA SHEARER
Norma Shearer with the rough and the smooth:
The rough – Clark Gable in *A Free Soul* **(1931).**
The smooth – Tyrone Power.
Marie Antoinette **(1938).**

Norma Shearer was born in 1904 in Montreal, Canada, of Scottish father and English mother. When she won a beauty contest at fourteen her mother's ambitions for her turned towards the stage, and in the depression of 1920, she took Norma and her sister to New York, where eventually Norma found work as an extra. She was also modelling, which she claimed, taught her how to achieve the mobile facial expressions screen acting requires. But the key to her charm lay in her voice. Musical, very pleasing and low-pitched, it was a Stradivarius on which she played like a brilliant virtuoso. She had studied hard to conquer the microphone, and her sound debut, *The Trial of Mary Dugan* ('29), was one of the great personal successes of the year. In her determination lay her strength. In this respect she was like Joan Crawford; as rivals, their difference lay in the roles they were identified with. Shearer was a lady; Crawford a shopgirl who dreamt of being a lady.

At the height of Norma's popularity, the only rival for the roles she played was Irene Dunne. Dunne had been a musical comedy star on Broadway and was to become one of Hollywood's more versatile actresses, changing between put-upon heroines, pioneer women, musical stars and screwball comediennes with the greatest of ease. She was equally popular in whatever she played, and without seeming to be, was as aware as Crawford of the need to anticipate the public's

MG

desire for a change, and so hold their attention. She possessed the most captivating smile and the sauciest laugh and admirably portrayed a gallery of self-sustaining and controlled wives, sweethearts, mothers and genteel mistresses. She starred in the seminal woman's drama, *Back Street* ('31), directed by John M. Stahl; and made the baroque *Magnificent Obsession* with him in 1935 and *When Tomorrow Comes* in 1941. For Leo McCarey she was sophisticated, witty and romantic in the ultimate love story, *Love Affair*, opposite a broodingly magnetic Charles Boyer. Two people, both promised to someone else, meet aboard a luxury liner, fall in love, and decide to part when they return to New York, to find out if what they felt was more than a shipboard romance. They agree to meet in six months time at the top of the Empire State Building. On her way to meet him, she is struck down by a car and crippled. She does not tell him, refusing to be a burden. He feels let down. Months later they meet again when he comes to her apartment to bring her a bequest from his grandmother and discovers that she is crippled.

IRENE DUNNE

Irene Dunne and Robert Montgomery in *Unfinished Business.*

Irene Dunne and Cary Grant in *Penny Serenade* **(1941).**
With Charles Boyer in *Love Affair.*

The locations were glamorous – Naples, the French Riviera, New York, ocean liners; both sets of stars ideal, the direction flawless. Audiences wept and laughed and identified Irene Dunne with the high quality of the production. She starred in five excellent emotional dramas made by the literate and atmospheric John Cromwell and made one of her most famous films, *Penny Serenade*, for George Stevens. This teamed her with Cary Grant in a story of a young couple's love, marriage and divorce. Stevens's device for telling the story was beautifully simple: dividing their belongings, he comes across a pile of old records, each with memories that open into flashbacks of their life. The film was well served by its principals: not only Dunne but Grant too gave a performance of marvellous sensitivity. The smoothness with which she could slip from girlish reserve into a deeply involving emotion was only once better served, and that in a film for one of the quirkiest directorial geniuses in Hollywood, Gregory La Cava. She had secured her initial reputation with a film directed by him, *Symphony of Six Million* ('32), a Fannie Hurst saga of a doctor's dedication to the poor. With La Cava she made a film that surpassed all her previous work: *Unfinished Business* ('41). When it was made, America was about to enter a war, and escapist musicals or outright propaganda were the order of the day. An audience for the more serious theme of *Unfinished Business* was scarce. Miss Dunne, a naïve and sentimental country girl on a train to New York, meets, is seduced by and believes she is in love with and loved by an ambitious politician. They meet again by accident when he comes to an exclusive supper club where she has found work as a waitress. Deeply hurt to discover he is married to someone else, she agrees to marry his alcoholic younger brother, as a means of getting closer to the man she loves. The two find they have a beneficial effect on one another – he stops drinking and she finds her feelings of sympathy turning to love. Discovering that she was in love with his brother, and thinking she still is, he leaves her. Realizing that she loves the man he has become, she convinces him to give their marriage another try.

This subject was fraught with obvious pitfalls. La Cava directed with pace, delicacy of touch, and total lack of self-pity for his characters, yet its realism did not detract from its romantic flavour. Its insight into the life of two weak and lonely people (even though they were portrayed by two of Hollywood's most attractive players to take some of the drabness out of it) showed a very rare talent; the two stars, Dunne and Robert Montgomery, were at their peak. It is a film whose neglect is incomprehensible.

Audiences recognized and admired these heroines as a breed apart; they were usually beautiful as well as good, and their films projected that quality down to the last detail. Ann Harding, Irene Dunne, Shearer and Kay Francis stood for 'class'. Theirs were a superior body of films; scripts were more literate, costumes and decor in unobtrusive good taste; although their subjects were every bit as sentimental as any in this category. Dignity was the key-note, humour their saving grace.

The 30s added the serenely beautiful Madeleine Carroll to the ranks. An English rose, cool and elegant whether in the costume dramas she flattered with her decorous period beauty, or in North-West-Mounted Police sagas; and even remaining unruffled as the woman least likely to fall for Bob Hope's brand of humour in *My Favourite Blonde*.

The 40s added Greer Garson, who made her mark as Mrs Chips, and despite one gay excursion to show how relaxed and attractive she was before her importance began to weigh on her in *Pride and Prejudice*, made marriage (without the sparkle Myrna Loy brought to that state) a decidedly sticky affair as *Mrs Miniver*, *Mrs Parkington*, *Madame Curie* and Irene Forsythe in *That Forsythe Woman*.

Later in the same decade, another titian-haired beauty was imported to Hollywood, having already become one of England's finest young actresses, Deborah Kerr. She possessed to a very high sense the qualities one associates with English women as seen through the eyes of a foreigner; those genteel self-denying lovely ladies who appeared in the novels of Rose Macaulay and Graham Greene. In an adaptation of one of Graham Greene's works, *The End of The Affair* ('55) Kerr gave a superb performance. For most of her American career she was used, as 'nature's ladies' always are, to play chaste Princesses and Queens, early Roman Martyrs, romantic governesses and nuns. On the whole, this type was usually played by blondes; they were rarely allowed to hint at the erotic force that can lie beneath a lady-like exterior. For this there had to be brunettes.

This was Mary Astor's forte, as she brought class and style to women of character, without sacrificing the eroticism that ran so strongly through her work. In films like *Red Dust*; in *Dodsworth* as the American expatriate Edith Cartwright, who gives Sam Dodsworth the chance of building a new life for them both; as Black Michael's mistress, Antoinette, prepared to sacrifice herself to save his life in *The Prisoner of Zenda*, she easily dominated her scenes and the films. Harlow's good-natured blonde tramp in *Red Dust* was evenly matched against the restrained sexuality that seemed to inflame Astor even before Gable touched her, and was so potent when, caught in a downpour, Gable carried her drenched body in his arms, the white linen

MADELEINE CARROLL

The serenely beautiful Madeleine Carrol. An English rose, cool, elegant whether in the costume dramas she flattered with her decorous period beauty or in the North West Mounted Police sagas; even remaining unruffled as the woman least likely to fall for Bob Hope's brand of humour in *My Favourite Blonde.*

With Robert Donat in *The 39 Steps* **(1935).**

With Ronald Colman in *Prisoner of Zenda* **(1937).**

suit plastered against her skin, her hair hanging wet and lank.

Another brunette to achieve a notable popularity for a time as a sophisticated romantic heroine was Kay Francis. From the beginning of the depression through to the outbreak of war, she agonized in beautiful clothes over men in dinner jackets in situations that called for a straight face and a stiff chin. Lubitsch had used her dark elegance perfectly in his romantic comedy, *Trouble in Paradise* ('32), but it was in Tay Garnett's *One Way Passage* ('32) that she played the role that made her a great favourite with women. It co-starred her with the suavest and most sympathetic of leading men, William Powell. A couple meet in a bar in Shanghai. He toasts her beauty and, after drinking, breaks the stem off his champagne glass and lays it on the bar before her. Amused and attracted, she does the same and crosses hers on his. Aboard the boat taking them back to America, they meet again. What neither knows is that both are doomed. She is incurably ill; he is a prisoner, sentenced to death. As they fall in love, neither can tell the other. The boat stops for a day by a tropic island. By a trick he gets to go ashore with her, while the Detective guarding him remains behind. He has an opportunity to escape but realizes that he cannot leave her. Docking in New York, she overhears two people discussing his case and understands why he had suggested they part. Her heart beating fast, the excitement almost too much for her to take, she sees him before he leaves. They arrange to meet, six months later, on New Year's Eve. As he disappears from view, she collapses and dies. On New Year's Eve, three of the people who had known all the details, the detective, his wife and the doctor, meet in a bar. At the stroke of midnight there is the burst of breaking glass. The bartender looks down amazed. On the table lying crossed on each other, are the stems of two champagne glasses.

Like *History Is Made At Night* and *Love Affair*, and later still, *Casablanca*, *One Way Passage* is one of those miraculous films in which fiction becomes poetry. Such movies struck a responsive nerve in a public fighting out of the Depression and later, in the midst of a war. The key to all their problems was Love.

For the rest of her career, Kay Francis played variations on the same theme; towards the end she began to look dehydrated from all that controlled passion.

It was the *Exotics* who starred in some of the wilder bursts of movie love, and the *Furies* – Barbara Stanwyck and Jennifer Jones, Gene Tierney and Gloria Grahame – whose passions produced some of the classics of the erotic cinema. There were few actresses as mysterious as Marlene Dietrich or as ravishing as Hedy Lamarr when they were around. Catherine Deneuve must be the most placid and Danielle Darrieux the most chic. In between and around them are others as fascinating, though of lesser stature, like Viveca Lindfors and Genevieve Page; some, like the strikingly gifted Jean Simmons and the evergreen Merle Oberon, are difficult to place in one category or the other. The successful Exotic was one who had been re-constructed in Hollywood for the mass market. Their accents were kept, though blurred to make identification difficult; their European sophistication was explained by giving them characters who arrive with a past

A favourite in the 30s, Greer Garson. Mary Astor in *Dodsworth*.

Kay Francis, Herbert Marshall and Miriam Hopkins in *Trouble in Paradise*. In 1932 these three were generally considered the 'ideal couple' because Lubitsch could get away with anything!

stamped on their brow. That's what being an Exotic meant to Hollywood – A Past. Futures were doubtful propositions for them; death or another port of call were usually the only alternatives. 'Only God and I know what is in my heart' was the song of the freed slaves in Robert Hichen's novel, 'The Garden of Allah'. Beautiful, wealthy and lonely, Domini Enfilden hears it out in the Sahara Desert, where she has returned to find solace. A world of heart-break and pain that can only be measured in the grains of sand blowing through the desert, or by a look in the eyes of the exotic. It was perfect casting when Marlene Dietrich played it in the Technicolor re-make of 1936. She had had long practice in looking and suggesting, under the supreme practitioner at making appearances deceptive, Josef von Sternberg. In some of the films directed by him, Dietrich became the screen's purest romantic transfiguration – as in *Morocco*, *Dishonoured*, *Shanghai Express* and that truly baroque tale of mother love, *Blonde Venus*. She rarely came from a specific place, but rather from a nebulous somewhere. Shanghai Lily was a white woman Captain Harvey first knew in England, but with that accent, she wasn't English. And although Dietrich was German, Lily's former name, Madeleine, is not a German one. The two meet again on the *Shanghai Express* – a train in transit is a country where all meet on an equal footing. In *Dishonored*, Dietrich, a Viennese streetwalker recruited to spy for her country, falls in love with her Russian enemy. Sentenced to die as a traitor by the firing squad, she refuses the uniform in which she served her country, preferring instead the one in which she served her countrymen. The bond that unites the legion of women who serve love has no national boundaries. In *The Blue Angel*, *Scarlet Empress* and *The Devil is a Woman*, on the other hand, she was the romantic antithesis: a chilling incarnation of dreams turned to ashes, a put-down of romantics as sentimental fools deserving of their degradation. Dietrich's beauty in all of these films is continuously surprising in its variety, Sternberg using her face as a mirror for the souls she encounters. After the termination of their partnership in 1935, Dietrich was used as a romantic exotic in several films but best of all, by Frank Borzage in *Desire* ('36). Unlike Garbo, Dietrich does not transcend her material without a director who knows how to use her. Both Boleslawski and Jacques Feyder left her to her own reputation, but Borzage made her part of the poetic rotation that is the special characteristic of his work.

Viveca Lindfors, one of the great beauties of her generation.

Kay Francis in *One Way Passage*.

Lubitsch was credited with personally supervising the production of *Desire* and the plot was the sort he liked, but there can be no doubt that the feeling that gives the film its romantic flavour is due to Borzage. Throughout, Dietrich is radiantly photographed, with a softness missing in her last few films with Sternberg – for Borzage understood well how a lover sees his beloved. Only one of her later films also came under the heading of exotic, René Clair's *Flame of New Orleans* ('41). This was a champagne cocktail. Everything was kept bubbling, as light as air, fragrant as a tree in blossom, fragile as Venetian glass. Clair laced with true Gallic wit and charm the Hollywood largesse at his disposal: shoulders were shrugged; eyebrows imperceptibly raised; drawing-room doors closed in the afternoon;

wedding gowns trailed through the streets and were found floating (but empty) on the waterfront. Dietrich could not have been bettered as the social-climbing gold digger who loses her heart to a sailor and runs off with him instead of marrying the millionaire she had fooled successfully. The film is all nuance, to be sipped slowly and not drained at one sitting.

The European Cinema had no comparable equivalent for Hollywood's *Exotics*. The success of both Dietrich and Garbo brought (among others) Anna Sten from Russia via the German Film Studios, that used her for her emotional ability as much as her undeniable beauty. The three films she made for Goldwyn were highly romanticized. Even the first of these, *Nana*, changed Zola's beautiful butterfly, spawned on a dunghill, into a standard romantic heroine. What made *Nana* an attractive subject for Sten's American debut was her lethal sexual attraction, which audiences were meant to identify with Sten. Her next film was nearer home, Tolstoy's novel *Resurrection*. Because it had already been done twice, with Mexican actresses (Dolores Del Rio and Lupe Velez) each time playing the ill-treated Russian peasant, it was now called *We Live Again*. Although in Hollywood terms Tolstoy's complicated tale of a man's conscience became just another story of a man's sin and a woman's payment, Rouben Mamoulian's understanding direction of what was left of the book made a film enjoyable to look at. Sten had an earthiness and a sensual beauty like Ingrid Bergman's, but too-clever lighting reduced her to the merely glamorous. King Vidor directed her in her last film for Goldwyn, *The Wedding Night* ('35), and her love scenes with Gary Cooper had Vidor's sprawling gorgeousness and emotional wallop. So did the melodramatic climax, enabling her to die by falling down a flight of stairs before her hateful marriage could be consummated.

Anna Sten had an earthiness and a sensuality like Ingrid Bergman's, but too-clever lighting reduced her to the merely glamorous.

It never fails to surprise me to remember that Hedy Lamarr's initial claim to fame was for the exposure of her nude body in the Czech film *Ecstasy* ('33), since her subsequent reputation rests solely on her face. Not just shopgirls, but almost every brunette star in Hollywood tried to copy it, including Joan Crawford and Joan Bennett. For a time, after her sensational appearance in *Algiers*, Lamarr wandered through films – *Lady of the Tropics, I Take This Woman, Come Live With Me* – some better than others, a femme-fatale in all of them, whose beauty launched men on a disastrous course of action. John Cromwell, who directed *Algiers*, Victor Fleming who directed her in *Tortilla Flat* (in which she was surprisingly effective though wildly miscast as a superstitious and highly emotional Mexican cannery worker), and of course, Cecil B. De Mille, whose films belonged in the same category as her beauty, were all able to use her to great effect. Lamarr was fathomless, in her actions or her motives. Close-ups revealed little, serving primarily as a homage to her beauty and to mystify us.

MARLENE DIETRICH
Dietrich and Gary Cooper in *Desire*.
Dietrich and Charles Boyer in *Garden of Allah*.
The Flame of New Orleans.

It was tricky work to be an exotic in the 40s. There was a war on and much of what had been exotic was now alien. American movies were either devoted to extolling the bravery of the decent ordinary men and women of their beleaguered allies or depicting the enemy and his mate as brutes. A small pistol hidden beneath a silken scarf is one thing, but the role of a freedom-fighter, roughing it in the hillside, was not in Lamarr's range. As an alluring priestess in an Oriental Temple she was believable; as a gun-toting heroine of the resistance, she would not have been. Her beauty was alien to reality.

Thus the exotic gave way to a new European type, needed to symbolize the good people over there: Women, who by their devotion, patience, resilience, courage, sacrifice and restrained sex-appeal, were worth defending. Greer Garson did her bit for the English wives and mothers. Dietrich went off to entertain the troops fighting at the war-fronts of the world, and Lamarr drifted into limbo for a spell.

But a new symbol *was* found – the radiantly beautiful Swedish actress Selznick had imported in 1939 to re-create in America her success in the Swedish film *Intermezzo* – Ingrid Bergman. In every respect she fitted the saintly ideal people wanted, though it would eventually rebound on her; but that came much later. Her beauty was fresh and pure. Lubitsch called her a big peasant. Translated that meant she was natural. Her accent had the Swedish lilt Garbo had already made familiar. Despite her height and solid build, she excelled in roles demanding spiritual quality. She had a delightful humour, though given few comedies to do.

As the Spanish Loyalist peasant girl Maria in *For Whom The Bell Tolls*; as the ambiguous heroine of Hitchcock's black thriller *Notorious*; and in her finest hour, asking Sam to 'Play it again' in the bitter-sweet love story *Casablanca*, Bergman became every man's ideal.

Casablanca, rightly a classic, came about by accident. Even Bergman's casting: first choice had been Hedy Lamarr, who turned it down, with good reason. The script gave no indication of what the film would be. Bergman has herself told how the script was being written while they were shooting, and that it was not until the last day that she or her co-stars, Humphrey Bogart and Paul Henreid, had any idea of how it would end. Hungarian-born Michael Curtiz, who directed *Casablanca*, would not at first have seemed the likely man to create this masterpiece, and Warner Bros. was not a studio geared to a romantic tradition in film making. Actresses complained of the dearth of stories there for them to do (though Bette Davis had an enviable career playing gutsy parts in powerful films). *Casablanca* profited from the doubt that surrounded the filming. The location was exotic, a Middle East trouble spot, held by the Free French and last refuge for expatriates fleeing from the invading Germans, hoping to buy forged passports that would lead them to freedom in America; an air of encroaching danger; beautiful women and desperate men; acts of patriotism and cowardice; the actors' uncertainty about the script projected itself into the people's uncertainty about being able to escape, about deciding between love and duty, and honour. Cynical, embittered Bogart; idealistic, rapturous Bergman, and a haunting song that bound them together, 'As Time Goes By', became a once-in-a-generation experience that belonged to the movies. Each viewing retains that air of unpredictability. It remains the film Bergman will always be remembered by.

Romantic gestures cling to Bergman; the child she had by the Italian director while still married to her Swedish doctor husband; her dignity under the furious outburst of abuse hurled at her by the Americans for destroying the image in which they had encased her; her growth as an artist and her brilliant come-back served as the ingredients for a legend.

After the war, a new, contemporary quality was introduced to most genres and types, and the Exotic was no exception. Now the mystery in Bergman's eyes was recognized as the traumatic experience of having lived through a war-torn Europe. Viveca Lindfors, another Swedish actress, strikingly lovely and forceful, and the rough-edged, capable Hildegarde Knef, still young, but with a knowledge of life bought for a price that could only be hinted at, stepped around the rubble of Berlin. Lindfors, an intelligent actress, played other roles besides – sad Spanish Queens and Gypsy sweethearts – but escaped being typed, and stardom with it. Knef's fatalism was too harsh, her range too confined, and few films used her properly.

The realism of the 50s spelled death to exotic allure – for a time. Busts became fashionable – so did a last burst of infantilism in love goddesses and other types. Child-women, all knowing, were their rivals for attention – Italy produced the former, France the latter. Françoise Arnoul, Dany Robin, Cecile Aubrey, and a string of girls all looking like Brigitte Bardot, pouted their way across films and magazine covers, but could hardly be called exotic or romantic. There was one foreign star working at this time who breathed romance in everything she did: Danielle Darrieux – *la vraie Parisienne*. From the

Ingrid Bergman in *Casablanca*. 'Here's looking at you, kid' – the famous last line.

Cary Grant and Ingrid Bergman in *Notorious* – two people who deserved each other.

Hedy Lamarr in *White Cargo* (1942). *Algiers.*

flicker of an eyelid to the crease of her brow or the pucker of her pretty French mouth, nothing she did was ever too much.

Working with Ophuls, Danielle Darrieux was perfect. Her career had been at a post-war ebb when her collaboration with the great director began. Her work for him re-established her critically as well as on a popular level, in France and abroad. As a pretty young thing in the 30s she had an international success with Charles Boyer, as the ill-fated lovers of *Mayerling*, and came to Hollywood to make one film, *The Rage of Paris* ('38). In the 50s she made several films in Hollywood, including a Jane Powell musical, *Rich, Young and Pretty* (playing her French mother), and a double agent opposite James Mason in the slick thriller, *Five Fingers*. Although Annabella, Simone Simon and Michele Morgan had longer American careers, it is Darrieux who, more than any other French actress, typified the romantic, romanticized image of the chic Parisienne, utterly feminine, charmingly trivial, deliciously vulnerable and ultimately obtainable.

Hildegarde Knef.

'For the female of the species is more deadly than the male.'
Rudyard Kipling.

There was something wild and romantic to the way these screen heroines fought, loved, killed and died. Often the romance in films starring a Barbara Stanwyck, Gloria Grahame or Jennifer Jones, lay in their person. Tragedy seemed to stalk them almost from the moment the credits had finished and an ominous chord in the background score prepared us for their first entrance. Because the femme fatale proved to be fatal to herself, it turned her from merely erotic into a romantic image. One was rarely disappointed. Barbara Stanwyck gave an interview when she first began to make a mark in films, in which she was quoted as saying 'I've had to push every gate that ever opened to me'; and that could be the epitaph for the heroines she specialized in for over thirty years in more than seventy-five films.

Some stars become popular as types that are later found to be contrary to their own personality – the shy private Rita Hayworth and the torrid *Gilda* Hayworth of her films for one, Ingrid Bergman for another, and Jennifer Jones who belongs among the screen's great Furies, as well. But in most cases, it is an aspect of themselves that the camera magnifies and the public identifies with. Gary Cooper in private was apparently the model of the man he was on-screen – a gentle knight without armour. The larger than life personality of Bette Davis triumphed on film in roles that took advantage of her outsize talent.

Danielle Darrieux.

A similar overlap can be seen in Barbara Stanwyck's career. Frank Capra, who directed her in the film that made her famous, *Ladies of Leisure* ('30), described her in his biography as 'one of those women one falls in love with at first sight'. In her portrayals, she was the screen's first active feminist. Society was the villain in Stanwyck's films, marring her early life; so when first we see her, the mould has cooled and become ironclad.

Jennifer Jones too, though earthier, more sensuous by far than Stanwyck's almost sexless furies, loved with a passion that invariably placed her beyond the pale – Pearl, the half-breed girl in *Duel in The*

Sun with her wild lover on the craggy mountain covered with their blood, gives and gets her peace from the barrel of a rifle in the shoot-out to end all shoot-outs. Or so one thought till Vidor, who directed the film, topped it with another, that had Jones as Ruby – the woman who tamed a town, man by man and sin by sin – *Ruby Gentry*.

Invariably, the heroines they portray end in an orgy of self-destruction. Human reason can explain the causes leading up to the tragedy in some instances but faced with the motivations of a Bacchae becomes inadequate. For example, Gene Tierney in *Leave Her To Heaven* – killing her husband's crippled brother, even bringing on her own miscarriage and in a final stroke, planning her suicide so that the blame rests on her younger half-sister, so that none of them can come between her and the husband she so possessively loves and wishes to keep even in death. Gene Tierney's plastic beauty lent itself to many shifting moods with fluid grace, enthralled even as she repulsed under John Stahl's spaciously composed direction. It's a hot summer noon on an open lake, the sunglasses hiding her eyes create the effect of a reverse negative of a face behind a mask as her husband's crippled brother looks up at her. He had been encouraged by her to swim beyond his strength, and gets cramp, and sinks. His pleas for help fall silent on her ears until she's sure he's gone. Later, her husband's concern and enthusiasm for their unborn child raises a threat to their closeness in her mind, and she forces the miscarriage by throwing herself down the stairs. The rights and wrongs of such consuming passion are in no doubt, but there's no denying the ruthless grandeur of her actions. Gene Tierney seemed to be governed by laws beyond her control – she was 'possessed' but could sometimes resolve it, happily, through love.

Gene Tierney.

Most of Stanwyck's memorable heroines were tragic. Had they lived now her puritan missionaries – grasping, amoral *Baby Face*, unwed mothers, pioneer women, her *Ladies of Leisure* and *The Miracle Woman*, defying exploitation of their sex by others, yet having to fall back on sex as their only weapons – would have found a cause in today's Women's Lib. The anguish one read in their faces was genuine and terrifying. Edward Albee's vitriolic, aged but ageless, shrew in *Who's Afraid Of Virginia Woolf* is like a compendium of all of Stanwyck's best roles, and by right, she was the only American actress who could have given the role in the film version any sense. Here was a woman who still clawed and spat because she once had to, and now, no longer knew how to stop. Without a cause to expend this tragic energy on, she turns it on herself. In this sense, Stanwyck's career is a tragic waste of a great talent. She, who was so well equipped to fight reality, was destroyed by clichés and bogged down in soap-operas.

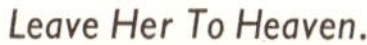

Leave Her To Heaven.

Born Ruby Stevens in Brooklyn, Stanwyck couldn't have been more American. Because, on the whole, she never fought for showy roles in important films, Stanwyck's reputation is cumulative, and has few such signposts as her contemporaries notched up. Her career was long, steady and respectable but instead of giving her Medeas and Electras, she was often in roles it is hardly likely anyone else of her stature wanted. Stanwyck seemed to accept roles that limited her

BARBARA STANWYCK
With Fred MacMurray in *Double Indemnity* **(1944).**
With Robert Ryan in *Clash By Night* **(1952).**

ROBERT TAYLOR

The Cagneys and Gables of the 30s found their reincarnation in Paul Newman, Steve McQueen and Clint Eastwood.

career while the woman she played on the screen seemed to seethe from similar injustice.

Only once or twice did she have a director and a film that could stand on its own, the romantic comedy Preston Sturges starred her in, *The Lady Eve* and an earlier one he scripted, *Remember The Night*, and Billy Wilder's *Double Indemnity*. In *The Lady Eve*, at the fade-out, we can almost believe that she has found happiness with Henry Fonda's innocent anthropologist who can tell one snake in the grass from another but is baffled by the ones on two legs. In James R. Cain's tale of murder and greed, with a script by Raymond Chandler and dialogue to file her nails on, she wore a blonde wig, a bracelet on her left ankle, and without an ounce of sympathy for the character, made Phyllis Dietrichson a classic study of the kind of woman who is driven by forces only her own death can still and for whom love, like Wedekind's *Lulu*, comes on a knife's edge or the point of a gun.

More sentimental was the film directed by Douglas Sierck and produced by the master craftsman of the women's picture, Ross Hunter – *All I Desire* ('52). The story of Naomi, who'd left her husband and children years ago because of an involvement with another man and the excitement offered her by the theatre and who now, older but still beautiful, tries to come home – to a husband bitter but still in love with her, to children who are grown and divided over her, to another woman who has been like a substitute mother to the children. Just when there is a chance of reconciliation, the other man tries to take advantage of their past affair. Here, once again, was the Stanwyck whom society could not forgive for striving for something better than her lot, but with a poignancy to which her reputation, her candour, her steel grey hair lent an enormous charge of emotion. After all, when a star has been around as long as Stanwyck, her films and life become part of a vast Thesaurus, cross-referenced to her other films, to films within the genre, and to our knowledge of her private life over the years.

There is nothing like frustration and repression to unleash the most powerful erotic forces in the soul or on the screen. This was the power of Gloria Grahame. She exuded neither sense of peace nor fulfilment; her challenge to the male ego was totally erotic. Like Stanwyck, though for different reasons, she too was an outsider. Unlike Stanwyck it was not self-doubt or neurotic flaws in her character that brought her to her doom; she came to it as the only real freedom. She had this quality whether playing gangsters' molls, unsatisfied housewives – *The Cobweb, The Bad And The Beautiful* – she won an Oscar for her role in the latter, as nightclub songbird, or scheming murderesses (*Sudden Fear* and *Human Desire*). For that matter, she is the only actress to face up to one of Crawford's most baleful stares in *Sudden Fear* without flinching, only brushing her hand across her face as if an insect had touched on it. On the whole, her roles rarely achieved absolute success, since there were few allowances for the threat she presented to the censor-clasped climate of her stardom. By the time the climate of conduct in movies became freer, with the influx of European films, she was off the screen. Her later roles became sparse and spaced far apart. The public lost track and the

Jennifer Jones, earthier, more sensuous by far than Stanwyck's sexless furies, loved with a passion that invariably placed her beyond the pale – as Pearl, the half-breed girl in *Duel In The Sun* or as *Ruby Gentry* – the woman who tamed a town, man by man, sin by sin.
Gone To Earth **(1951).**
With Montgomery Clift in *Indiscretion Of An American Wife* **(1954).**

GLORIA GRAHAME
The Grahame 'look'.

With Glenn Ford in ***Human Desire*** **(1955).**

roles she played did not take her ageing into consideration. But in a way, I doubt that her career would have been much different had she worked in a later period – except as a vamp. She doesn't really fit easily into any of the conventions, even of the love goddesses. Like Louise Brooks she was unique and difficult to cast. She looked great with cleavage, sexy on sheets. Placed on a pedestal in the middle of the desert she would not appear remote. She was a self-destructive fuse the man ignited when he kissed her. Like the divas of the early Italian Cinema, she went down with the male she destroyed. Perhaps classic tragedies would have given her suitable parts. In their place, Fritz Lang, who had already shown long ago with *Metropolis* ('25) his understanding of the bitch-goddess, and later, in such 40s' works as *Scarlet Street* and *The Woman In The Window*, with woman as a force of fate, directed her brilliantly in two films in the 50s – *The Big Heat* and *Human Desire*.

Gloria Grahame has of course played other roles as well: comedies; a musical even, as a very larky Ado Annie who 'Cain't say no' with such zest in *Oklahoma*; and she has been sympathetic and vulnerable as in De Mille's *Greatest Show On Earth*, all of which merely proves that she is an actress of considerable talent. As a matter of fact, only one actress in recent years, a contemporary, comes to mind as having a similar magnetism on film. The French actress, gliding like a fascinating serpent through the boudoirs of historical dramas and gallic romps, Genevieve Page. She too exudes an erotic force with romantic recklessness; whether as Liszt's discarded mistress, or a Castilian Princess who'd rather see El Cid dead than happy, or as the lesbian Madame of the brothel in Buñuel's *Belle De Jour* – she sparkles with a rare and carnal beauty.

As it is, Grahame's laurels were gained by great work in minor films and supporting parts in the important ones. She was lucky to have two films by Minnelli and two masterpieces by Fritz Lang, the American version of the French classic, La Bête Humaine, *Human Desire*, and his gangster thriller, *The Big Heat*. The latter has become notorious as the film in which a sadistic killer (Lee Marvin) hurls a scalding pot of boiling coffee into Gloria's face. She takes her revenge and meets her death in the final blow-out. But in the Zola story she had her greatest moment. I can see even now, that naked, glistening face, waxen smooth, curiously synthetic at times and motionless like temple carvings of 'bitch' goddesses with only those old eyes, looking too cynical, too knowing, from out of it.

Love Goddesses by comparison are a harmless bunch – masculine ideals of the desirable female which women, who controlled to a large degree what Hollywood produced, went along with and copied. Harlow and Lake, Lana Turner and Rita Hayworth, and the sublime catalyst that was Marilyn Monroe stepped into the fantasies Clara Bow once filled. Like Bow and Bara before her, their private doings became part of the evolution of their myth. They were the domestic equivalent of the exotic imports – a bit tawdrier, a little less glamorous. The 40s especially needed a domestic substitute for the foreign femme fatale, and the Love Goddess became the new substitute. In fact she was only the good-hearted sex-star they knew in the 30s,

Harlow as an amiable tramp revolutionized the image of the sex goddess from the brunette vamp to the alluring blonde.

Lizbeth Scott – when she spoke she sounded like a famished tiger.

The fallen angel – Veronica Lake of the hair.

pretending to a world-weariness, though cynicism came harder and mystery not at all. They were party girls in tight sweaters, the kind boys looked at as they walked by, and other girls pointed at enviously and giggled about cruelly.

The publicity men of the studios for whom they worked garnished them in tags they hoped would become national catch lines – some did. Harlow had been the 'Platinum Blonde'; Ann Sheridan had 'Oomph', Carole Landis was the 'Ping', Bacall was 'The Look' and gravel-throat Scott was 'The Threat'; Veronica Lake was the girl with the hair, Dorothy Lamour the one in the sarong; and Lana Turner was the 'Sweater Girl'. They didn't know what to make of Ava Gardner, though adverts for *The Barefoot Contessa* called her 'the world's most beautiful animal', but her allure needed no tricks to get attention, neither did the symbol of all such sirens of her decade, Rita Hayworth, who became the first Love Goddess.

The power of publicity, especially in regard to Love Goddesses, had come in with Theda Bara. Now it came into its own. Love Goddesses were nearly all promoted by publicity, especially between films, to appear to be that which they seemed in their roles. This was accepted until well into the 50s, with Marilyn Monroe and Brigitte Bardot, and reached its apotheosis in a burst of blood and lunacy that surrounded the Lana Turner-Johnny Stompanato affair. Here was a real life drama that looked very much like the plots of yet another of Miss Turner's films, and to most people, the Lana Turner crying on the witness stand must have seemed like a public dress-rehearsal for one of her films. For so well and so often had she played the same part and suffered the same misunderstandings on the screen in films like *Johnny Eager* ('41), *The Postman Always Rings Twice* ('46), and *The Flame And The Flesh* ('54), that it was only natural that she should expect and receive our sympathy when life emulated her roles. Proof that Love Goddesses were expected to be in real life what they seemed to be in films was their increased popularity, while those that failed to support this illusion stood less chance of keeping their popularity.

LANA TURNER
With Robert Taylor in *Johnny Eager* **(1941).**
The Postman Always Rings Twice **(1945).**

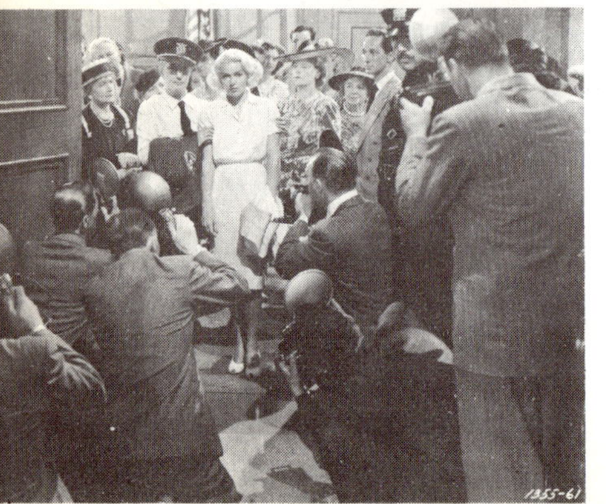

Subsequent to the trial, Lana Turner returned to films a bigger star than before, in a triumphant trio for producer Ross Hunter, of luxuriously mounted tales of suffering and repentance in diamonds and furs. The most famous, *Imitation Of Life*, was the first film she made after the trial. In *Portrait In Black*, she was the adulterous wife of a sadistic, crippled millionaire. Lastly, in the finest performance of her career, as *Madame X* ('65), she played the archetypal mother, whose life is ruined because she is the sort of woman of whom the worst is always thought, though she is innocent.

The era of the Love Goddess virtually ended with the death of Monroe in 1962. As a substitute for the exotic, Jeanne Moreau had the allure of sheets in need of the laundry. Liz Taylor appeared to confuse passion with weight. The trend towards youth, liberation and self expression gave us some actresses but no new heroines, sirens, or ladies. And the furies, once they began to speak their minds, were happier but decidedly dull. As for today's star women, it will take the future to reveal where they are heading.

SOME MEN

Whatever the woman's role was prior to Women's Lib, in movies she was triumphantly all. The man she loved she sacrificed for; she bore and supported his child (preferably a boy so she could suffer some more when he grew up). Her life revolved around men and children, for whom she would rise to the heights or sink to the depths, an emotional elevator, and the story was seen from her point of view.

The male stars were naturally not enthusiastic about playing second fiddle to the heroine. There were of course (and needed to be) a whole school of actors who gained popularity as leading men to the great female stars: Warren William, George Brent, Herbert Marshall, Sterling Hayden, Barry Sullivan among many, but only rarely did one of them, like Van Heflin, escape to establish himself as a star in his own right. It was rare for an established male idol to co-star with one of the screen's goddesses after having left those roles behind. Garbo's leading men were rarely of her box-office standing. The same applied to the partners of actresses like Ruth Chatterton, Claudette Colbert, Bette Davis, *et al.*

At M.G.M., Clark Gable and Robert Montgomery balked at being used to support the female stars around whom the studio revolved, especially since their popularity often surpassed that of the women. When Gable played Rhett Butler in *Gone With The Wind* he was the most popular star in the world, but back at his home studio, he was still being billed after Shearer and Crawford, though neither's pull was anywhere near his at the time. As a whole, the supporting role was not conducive to a man's ego, as Joan Crawford's husbands and co-stars would bear out, and she herself admitted in interviews. Both Doug Fairbanks Jr. and Franchot Tone played second fiddle to their wives in their films. And while there have been some very popular romantic stars like those tough softies – James Cagney, Humphrey Bogart, George Raft, John Garfield, Alan Ladd and William Holden – except for rare excursions into the woman's realm (Bogart in *Casablanca*, Garfield in *Humoresque*, or Ladd in *When Tomorrow Comes*) the films they starred in do not fit into the romantic cinema despite their own popularity as romantic heroes.

Unlike the female of the species, as different as they are many, the men, on the whole, have been straightforward, more or less divided between the rough and the smooth, the foreign lover and the homespun dreamer.

Clark Gable, with the big ears that stuck out from the side of his head and the cocky grin that spread roguishly across his handsome face, was rough. He became 'The King', slapping women around with one hand and defending them with the other, and they liked him for it because at heart, they knew, he was just a kid. Cary Grant was smooth, from the top of his immaculately combed and cut hair to the marrow of his narrow-collar good looks, the faultlessly creased and always stylishly elegant suits down to his spotless casuals. The best restaurants, the right wines; a ballroom dancer and a *bon vivant*; yet with a reserve that was attractive and hinted at strength should the need arise.

CLARK GABLE

It Happened One Night **(1934) – a puzzled Clark Gable, having exhausted his means of hitching a ride, gives way to the feminine wiles of runaway heiress, Claudette Colbert.**

Nearly a quarter of a century later, Gable was still taming and teaming with the screen's greatest beauties. Here he was with Ava Gardner in the re-make of *Red Dust*, *Mogambo* (1953).

He was also a versatile actor, though best remembered and admired for his charming seduction of the screen's most elegant beauties for thirty years, keeping the romantic fires burning in both the old and the new generations who discovered him in the 50s all over again. He was excellent working with Alfred Hitchcock, who used his smoothness and congeniality as a deceptive veneer, behind which lurked potential psychopaths and homicidal maniacs (*Suspicion*), sado-masochists whose mental torture of the heroine is far more insidious than the actual threats on her life (*Notorious*), elegant Riviera crooks (*To Catch A Thief*) and harassed executives (*North By Northwest*). Hitchcock of course played the same perverse double game in his casting of James Stewart, the gangly boy next door, whose home-spun sentimental nature was just an appealing front for a voyeur in a wheelchair in *Rear Window*, and the necrophile in *Vertigo*. Unlike the women exotics, few foreign male stars except for Charles Boyer made much of an international impression after the coming of sound, except as perhaps stereotypes. Nowhere near the scale of a Gary Cooper or the sweet and sour Humphrey Bogart, or any of the moody, rebellious heroes who first came on strong in the late 30s with John Garfield. Their sensitive streak was further probed later in the next decade by dreamy, doomed young Montgomery Clift and exploded into the centre of focus in the 50s with Brando and James Dean.

America's romantic ideal, who was as beautiful as any of his leading ladies.
Montgomery Clift in *The Big Lift* **(1950).**

The men, not always as colourful, but steady and durable, lasted into the 60s; with the star system in tatters, they still magnetize more than ever – Clint Eastwood and Robert Redford, Paul Newman and Steve McQueen, stepping easily into the grooves first cut in the 30s.

When Clint Eastwood gives his wry smile, chewing on a cheroot and all the time aiming his rifle with deadly accuracy at the villain, it's Cooper and Gable all over again. About the only concession to current trends is their habit of taking off their clothes on screen, but even in that they had their progenitors in Fairbanks and Valentino. Other than that, they still keep their mouths shut and their secrets locked up inside themselves. What held true for Cagney or Bogart is also the code of conduct for Newman and McQueen – 'A man has to do what a man has to do'. Therein lies the appeal of the modern male as well as the old.

Humphrey Bogart and Lauren Bacall in *To Have And Have Not*. **The chemistry between them was noticeable from the first day of shooting.**

Steve McQueen, sullen and a loner, as *Bullitt* or *Nevada Smith* or the elegant Raffles-like criminal superman of *The Thomas Crown Affair* follows the same code of conduct, with his sexy grease-monkey face, and those cool blue eyes embedded in the weatherbeaten like-leather skin from which they seem simultaneously to mock and entreat, even as his creased forehead creases even more, and his lips tighten into an appearance of alienation from fellow warmth. It applies too to Robert Redford, the Sun-God, romantic even as an anti-hero in *Inside Daisy Clover*, and *The Candidate*; sex-symbol in the bedroom and the out-of-doors; reckless in his search for speed and sympathetic as the victim of society.

The backwoods dreamers of Barthelmess and Charles Ray, sensitive but capable, appealing to the sentimental corners of a woman's heart; and the poets and romantic misfits glimpsed behind the aggressive front of John Garfield, both found a perfect latter-day equivalent in Montgomery Clift. The feminine streak in men, rarely hinted at before, added a depth to him.

The sexual ambivalence, which played a sideline part in Clift's appeal to women, took centre stage a few years later, exploding on the screen in the brutish and vulnerable, sensuous, profoundly sexual personality of Marlon Brando in *A Streetcar Named Desire*. With him the Steppenwolf came out into the open. As Stanley Kowalski, swilling beer and reeking of sweat, he brutally terrifies and physically assaults his sensitive sister-in-law, and drives her into her only refuge, insanity. But he is *not* the Griffith villain any more. He is the hero. When he goes pleading, mewing like a baby for its mother, to ask his earth-wife to take him back, she does. The meek must die so the strong can live. The once-lonely wolf of the steppes, circling on the sidelines of the warmth, had with one big leap, stormed in and taken possession. In America the time was right for the taking. Physically of course Brando was cast in a heroic mould – it was the complex forces he brought with him that set him apart from the old guard. His strength lay where others had been weak. He carried the seeds that would flower into the liberated male of the 60s. Brando, and taking the type even further, James Dean, had to be the centre of everything with the people they loved and who loved them – not just husband and lover but brother, father, child and, if need be, woman as well. James Dean's death wish and romanticized sensitivity (it was not romantic while he lived) fitted more easily into the mythmaking that took place from the moment his racing car crashed and he died. The industry that sprang up to cash in on the necrophiliac craze that swept the world made sure that it lasted longer than it should have. Sex and speed, freedom and virility became synonymous with stars in cars and on motorcycles. Films extolling the erotic attraction in speed as well as the symbol of a man's last stand for freedom in a steadily encroaching urban society, became popular and are still with us – Paul Newman in *Winning*, Steve McQueen in *Le Mans*, Robert Redford in *Downhill Racer*, Burt Lancaster in *The Gypsy Moths* (sky diving), James Garner in *Grand Prix*, and Marlon Brando, where it all began, in *The Wild One*.

Brando, who filled the screen with a new male type, still fitted himself into some of the existing moulds as well – hero and lover (Napoleon in *Desirée*, and *Sayonara*) – and made typing more difficult, becoming a law unto himself. A new breed of actors appeared in his wake, but of them all, Paul Newman alone proved durable. Looking like a wholesome Brando, he passed for a rebel till the perennial types re-established themselves, when he turned out to be as old-fashioned and satisfying as the Gables and the Gregory Pecks; while Brando, still active twenty years later, is admired for being again the loner, the type he had once brought into the main arena.

The 50s was a burial ground for legends – they either died or (except for Grant) retired. Bogart, Cooper and Gable died. A lot of the types replenished themselves in the 60s, as I've tried to point out, but the women, who had been the surest barometers of the social scene, never found new stars to regain the old glories.

James Stewart and Kim Novak in *Vertigo*.

Mary Murphy and Marlon Brando in *The Wild One* **(1954).**

Robert Redford in *Little Fauss And Big Halsy* **(1971).**

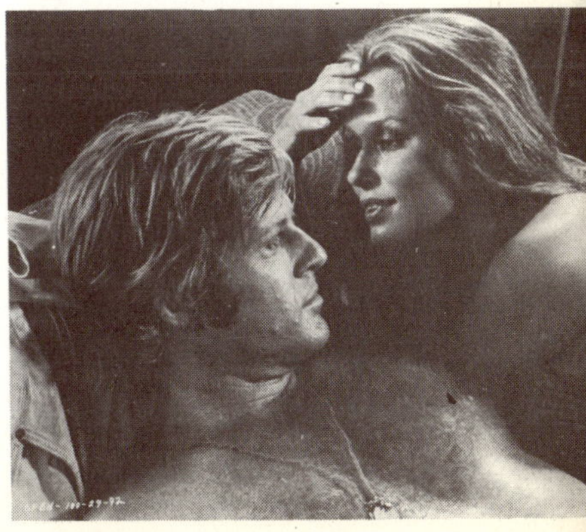

CHAPTER THREE

LOVE AFTER DEATH

Movies were born during the late years of the Victorian era and carried their conventions well into the twentieth century, especially in Anglo-Saxon countries, dominated by the Protestant ethic. As such, they fell heir to many tried-and-true theatrical conventions and, by the time the cinema had gained the respectability it took the stage centuries to acquire, these conventions had hardened into the rules of the various censorship codes. Not the least among them was the late-Romantic strain of love-beyond-the-grave present in song, poetry and dramatic literature, which the screen was to make its own with surprising ease. Another was the notion of love rewarded in the hereafter. D. W. Griffith gave us excellent examples of both in film strips that transcend through the beauty of their form their sampler morality and wistful naïveté.

But it was at the end of the First War that the stages of the world were to enjoy a revival of mystical themes on a grand scale. It was as if the theatre was attempting to erase the memory of the recent holocaust with some spiritual affirmation of its own, or to make a poetic escape into a world of durable values and feelings. What most of these plays and motion pictures suggested, sometimes almost subliminally, was a re-assuring continuity between life and afterlife, between generations, a way of refuting the very understandable cynicism of the post-war era. And so, in the West End and Broadway, *Death Takes A Holiday* thrived next to *What Price Glory?*, *Liliom* competed with *Journey's End*, and *The Return Of Peter Grimm* was running next door to *Gentlemen Prefer Blondes*. The former were the spiritual obverse of the latter, and, as was to be expected, in such fashions, the films were not very far behind.

Typical of the whole 'spiritual' trend which started during the First War was the play *Smilin' Through* by Jane Murfin and Jane Cowl, the latter a popular stage actress who shrewdly took a hand in fashioning star vehicles for herself. The play was a great success in 1919, and soon thereafter was beyond revival. The film adaptations – three between 1922 and 1941 – continued to carry its message of sentimental uplift to people and places beyond the reach of the stage. The story reads much clumsier than it actually plays. *Smilin' Through* is concerned with the undying love of the stalwart John Carteret for the beautiful, doomed Moonyean. On their wedding day, she is shot down at the foot of the altar by a rejected suitor. Years pass, and Carteret, now a lonely old recluse, is entrusted with the care of little Kathleen, niece of the woman he loved and lost. The child grows up to be an exact replica of Moonyean. She brings joy back into her guardian's life, even obtains his permission to marry a young man who turns out to be the descendant of her aunt's murderer. Carteret dies the gentle death reserved in this type of drama to those who remain forever faithful. He is reunited with Moonyean, both now eternally young, in the afterworld.

The 20s were already roaring when Norma Talmadge appeared in the silent film version of *Smilin' Through* which nevertheless became a runaway success. Its sentiment worked as an escape-hatch from the more cynical, materialistic outlook on love and life that prevailed at the time. The picture had the sort of faded, lingering charm found in

1934

such old songs as 'Just a Song at Twilight' (which, incidentally, was used as part of the score in the last remake). Throughout, the gossamer image of Miss Talmadge hovered in double exposure over the rest of the cast like a benign influence to guide the steps of young Kathleen, whom she also portrayed, and to warm up the cold, cold heart of old Carteret. All the film really lacked was sound to give aural life to the play's lines. Audiences who wanted to hear the heroine's dying breath along with her dying words – the well-remembered 'Isn't it a pity, John?' – were not disappointed by the sumptuous 1932 remake. Norma Shearer played the twin roles of Moonyean and Kathleen. The other-worldliness of the characters was preserved by Shearer's Pre-Raphaelite features and wraith-like deportment, even when this new version went easy on ectoplasmic apparitions, that is, until the conclusion when Moonyean summoned Carteret, played by Leslie Howard, to their eternal bliss. The most successful of all three versions was paradoxically produced on the eve of another World War. It had Frank Borzage as its director, which was already an advantage over Sidney Franklin who had directed the two previous versions; but most of all, it had Technicolor. A stain of scarlet gradually spreading over the immaculate, lacy bosom of Jeannette Macdonald set up, even without the help of words and music, a series of romantic resonances in our minds, something like the simile of the rose in medieval literature. One is not merely touched by Moonyean's untimely death but, at the same time, reassured that her maidenhood had been preserved forever.

Smilin' Through **(1932). Norma Shearer as Moonyean with Leslie Howard as John Carteret. (1923) Norma Talmadge as Moonyean.**

Jeanette Macdonald as Moonyean with Brian Ahearne in Frank Borzage's 1941 *Smilin' Through.*

Hollywood became expert at knocking off the capital R in Romantic agony, and substituting a sentimental fabrication, whose surface remained unruffled by anything disquietingly morbid. It would seem almost sacrilegous to refer to Moonyean's spirit as a ghost. In non-Western mythologies, however, like in the Japanese 'Tales of the Pale Moon after the Rain', the maiden princess who dies without ever having known carnal love is doomed to haunt the world of the living as an errant spirit. She is not quite the figure of horror that a Western mind presupposes – indeed, as portrayed by Machiko Kyo, she is an exquisite, ethereal creature – but nevertheless she is finally forced to yield her hold on the hero through religious exorcism.

One of the features of Victorian mystical romance, which lies at the heart of *Smilin' Through*, is its secularity, and until very recently, movies dreaded all but the most simplistic involvement with religion. The advocates of mystical fantasies were satisfied to reckon that 'spiritual' themes offered to the public served to counteract the materialistic drift of the period. Love after death, benevolent shades watching after lovers, filled the screen with clockwork regularity in the 20s and 30s, like Easter Sunday sermons admonishing a world in the grip of excess or chaos. But any of the darker, deeper meanings inherent in many of these films were usually smothered in period frills and Victorian attitudes. It took World War Two to update the genre, as with the highly effective *A Guy Named Joe* ('43) which audiences greatly responded to, at a time when many of these Americans had suffered the loss of a father, a son or a husband. People left the film – and others like *Here Comes Mr Jordan* ('41) – with an emotional reassurance of a not-too-different life after death.

The 30s appear now as *the* spiritual decade for the motion picture. It opened with an adaptation of Ferenc Molnar's international stage success *Liliom* ('30) made at Fox by Frank Borzage, which was followed three years later by a French version directed by Fritz Lang at

'Isn't it a pity, John?' whispers Moonyean as she slips into the other world just as she is about to wed the man she loves.

The phantom princess (Machiko Kyo) and the bewitched potter (Masayuki Mori), the lovers in *Ugetsu Monogatari* (Tales of A Pale & Mysterious Moon After The Rain) (1953).

Jeanette Macdonald and Nelson Eddy in *Maytime* (1938).

the outset of his exile, and also financed by Fox. The reason for this seeming extravagance being the different sensibilities of American and European audiences. Borzage's film played up the romance of the handsome cad whom no woman could resist, and who, falling reluctantly in love with an innocent girl, is then lured into crime by his need to provide for his wife and imminent child. Killed in his first hold-up, his soul is transported to heaven aboard a ghostly train. A kindly godhead decrees that he must return to Earth to perform one good deed, which turns out to be Liliom's heartfelt admission of his very real love for his wife and child. If love were all, as the song contends, Borzage's version would take the cup. Charles Farrell as Liliom was in line with the soft-core heroes of other Borzage films. Lang, the ironist, had Charles Boyer portraying the barker as a raffishly sexual creation who actually beats his wife, and adds some wonderful, sinister angels to whisk his soul to judgement. In certain scenes – as when the swaggering, youthful Boyer sings a lilting hurdy-gurdy tune by Franz Waxman to the limp-eyed Madeleine Ozeray – the Lang version could give Borzage's a romantic run for its money, before venturing into darker worlds. In the end, both versions agreed that, all in all, paradise was rather a forbidding place and certainly no match for the heaven-on-earth that love could create.

Liliom's celestial express reappears in the guise of a fog-bound steamer transporting a cargo of souls to the hereafter in *Outward Bound* ('30), adapted from a play by Sutton Vane. Among the passengers is a young couple of suicides (Douglas Fairbanks Jr. and Helen Chandler), ready to face any sort of divine punishment but separation from one another. The ship's steward is revealed as still another suicide, doomed to travel back and forth throughout eternity, collecting souls; but the lovers are spared such a dire fate by being sent back to Earth to live out their lives all over again. Despite the undistinguished direction of Robert Milton, this metaphysical *Grand Hotel* stuck to its fantasy guns and remained for the most part a grey, desolate nightmare. A World War Two remake, *Between Two Worlds* ('44), took an easier way out, making the story a dream of the lovers (now impersonated by Paul Henreid and Eleanor Parker) as they drift into unconsciousness and death in their gas-filled room. A bomb blast nearby shatters the window pane, reawakening in them the life force, a neatly contrived twist that in no way violated the admonitory tone of the original.

The sturdiest of poetic conceits, the giving of human form to Death, has supported many a successful film allegory, from Fritz Lang's *Der Müde Tod* to Ingmar Bergman's *The Seventh Seal*. But none is as romantic as the adaptation of a play by Alberto Casella, *Death Takes A Holiday* ('34), in which Death appropriates the handsome features, elegant clothes, monocle and decorations of a Continental prince (Fredric March) to walk unrecognized among ordinary mortals, and discover why they fear him. The mortals in this case are a more than ordinary party of aristocrats vacationing on the Italian Riviera, among them an elderly Count who gives Death a crash-course on the philosophy of love. Learning that love is the one thing worth living, let alone dying for, Death decides to try his hand at it, neglecting his duties as Last Summoner for three days – the horrible implications of which are carefully evaded. His first attempt fails, because the girl sees through his carnal disguise and recoils in horror. It is Grazia (Evelyn Venable), a girl suffering from a death-wish, who logically turns out to be Death's soul mate. Then, what would have been a dance of death becomes an elegant waltz, and a stroll in a moonlit garden serves as passage to Stygian darkness. Everything in the picture has been carefully arranged to take the sting out of death and put life in the hereafter.

Love continues to beckon from the beyond in *Maytime* ('37), as the disembodied voice of Nelson Eddy serenades Jeanette MacDonald. MacDonald, an old woman, sits by a flowering cherry-tree in her garden, reminiscing to a callow young girl about her career as a famous prima donna and her tragic love affair with Eddy, shot by a jealous impresario (John Barrymore in a most effective display of bravura). MacDonald has lived on for years and years, sustained by the memory of her love and the occasional encore from Eddy. At the end of her story – which in flashback forms the bulk of the picture – she appears to doze off. The youngster tiptoes away. Enter Nelson Eddy in double exposure; a young Jeanette rises from her seat and the reunited spirits join voices in a reprise of 'Will You Remember?', one of Sigmund Romberg's most enduring melodies, in a happy ending to end all happy endings. Lovers like these, according to the film, can only live happily ever after if they are dead.

The afterworld, then, is a dream landscape where the Victorian

The non-romantic hereafter: bureaucracy and fog in *Here Comes Mr Jordan* (1941). In the centre, Claude Rains, the angel-as-executive.

***A Guy Named Joe* (1943). Spencer Tracy and Barry Nelson as ghosts watch over Van Johnson, Irene Dunne and Ward Bond.**

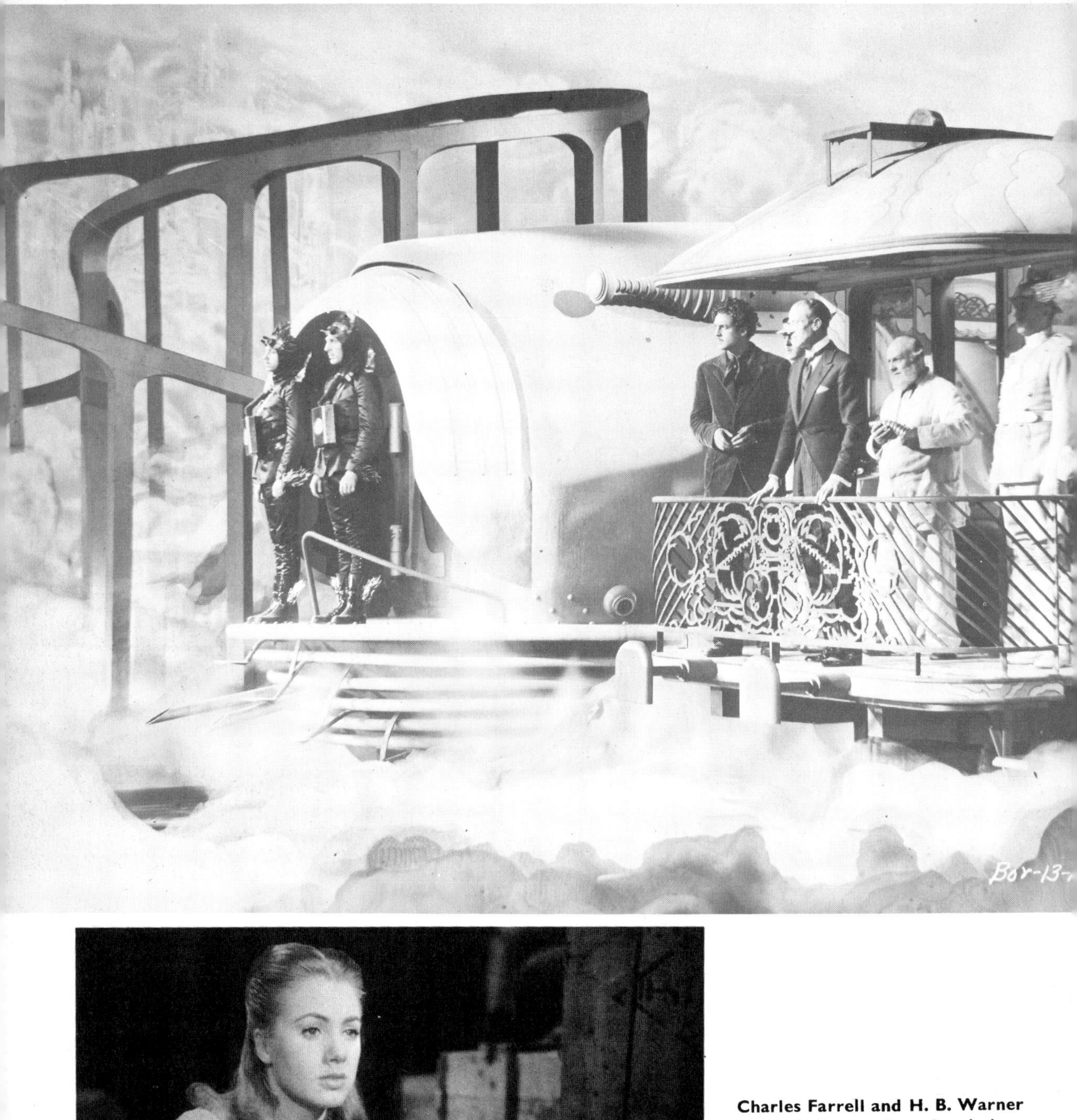

Charles Farrell and H. B. Warner on the heaven-bound train in *Liliom* (1930).
Gordon Macrae and Shirley Jones in *Carousel* (1956), the musical version of *Liliom*.

libido can be safely fulfilled, a place for lovers to meet in spirit while their bodies are kept apart elsewhere. Death functions either as release or confirmation of love everlasting, for instance, George du Maurier's *Peter Ibbetson*. Popular literature knows of no more ill-fated lovers than Peter and the Duchess of Towers, childhood sweethearts separated by life and reunited in another dimension while their corporeal selves waste away, hers in self-imposed seclusion, his in prison to which he has been sentenced after accidentally killing her villainous husband. Dying almost at the same time, they are restored to the luminous meadows of their childhood, surely one of the most crowded patches in heaven, where they will undoubtedly run into Macdonald and Eddy, but hopefully not into the jealous impresario or the late Duke of Towers. Despite the presence of Ann Harding and Gary Cooper in elegant settings and beautiful period costumes, the 1935 version could hardly disguise a basic lack of involvement with its subject, and Americans remained for once sceptical. Not so with the French who, more attuned to the surreal, dream-like quality of the film, hailed it as one of Hollywood's all-too-rare excursions into *l'amour fou*.

Outward Bound **(1930). Douglas Fairbanks Jr. and Helen Chandler as the lovers who have committed suicide.**
Between Two Worlds **(1944). The up-dated version of** *Outward Bound* **with Eleanor Parker and Paul Henreid as the desperate lovers about to commit suicide by turning on the gas.**

Du Maurier had received more congenial treatment in the John Barrymore version of his novel and play *Trilby*, aptly retitled *Svengali* and released in 1931. It is practically a case-book of repressed sexual attitudes, with its virginal heroine (who, nevertheless, poses in the nude), its weak and ineffectual hero (who is shocked by Trilby's occupation), and its demon lover (foreign, charismatic, reeking of sweat).

The original was adapted to the stage soon after its first appearance in 1893, and, in time, spawned no less than six movie versions. It also boasts some tortuously romantic passages, as when Svengali exerts his hypnotic influence on the guileless Trilby (Marian Marsh, almost too literally typecast): a close-up of eyes in a vulture-like face followed by a soaring crane shot over the roofs and gables of the Latin Quarter which comes to a stop on Trilby's garret as she prepares for bed. Her window is blown open as if by a sudden gust of wind. Another moment would have titillated our forefathers and as a matter of fact, still carries a strong whiff of suggestiveness. The hypnotist, attempting to bend Trilby to his amorous advances, merely succeeds in turning her into a distorted, mock-sensuous image of herself. Svengali retreats in disgust, muttering: 'My manufactured love . . . It's only Svengali talking to himself again.' He does, however, get the girl. Dying of a massive heart attack, his body consumed by the continued exertion of his powers, he summons the last of his strength to take Trilby with him to the grave 'O God, grant me in death what was denied to me in life . . .'. Barrymore had played Peter Ibbetson in his halcyon stage days and could still conjure up those dark romantic visions du Maurier so craftily concealed behind the facade of his melodramas.

The best example of the Demon Lover, however, is not Svengali but another popular Victorian image, that of Dracula the Vampire, the night visitor whose victims, mostly young and virginal, await restlessly under quilted covers in the sanctity of their middle-class bedrooms. Except for a first version made in Germany by F. W. Murnau and retitled *Nosferatu*, which transcended the theme of the Bram Stoker novel and became a very Germanic allegory of good and evil, subsequent adaptations in America and Britain retained and (of late) emphasized the romantico-sexual aspect of a foreign gentleman in evening clothes exerting a quite ungentlemanly power of seduction over women.

In 1934, an expensive advertisement in the 'Motion Picture Herald' proclaimed Hollywood's new allegiance to the past: 'And from a source not even the most critical can question, the vast storehouse of the world's favorite books!' Ready to be tapped lay the rich lode of Victorian literature. Apart from the odd Shakespearean adaptation, the past for the producers meant Dickens and Stevenson, Conan Doyle, Rider Haggard, Ouida, or Anthony Hope. But when Hollywood finally took a crack at a *bona fide* masterwork like Emily Brontë's *Wuthering Heights* it was not fully prepared to do it justice. A medium that could work wonders with minor literature was equally adept at reducing the complex terms of the Brontë book to the usual romantic imagery.

For the millions who did not know, nor care, about the original novel, the film became the epitome of romanticism in 1939. An idyllic interlude in the Yorkshire moors, supported by the lyrical score of Alfred Newman and the virtuoso camera-work of Gregg Toland, it starred the young Laurence Olivier, so handsome, dark and demonaic that he has imprinted his image in our mind, as the one and only Heathcliff. But, in every other respect, the picture was pure Daphne du Maurier. Gone was 'the hatred, conflict and horror' of the tale; gone was Heathcliff's near-blasphemous rage at Cathy's death; and gone too, although shot and discarded, was Heathcliff's death, sprawled over Cathy's snow-covered grave. Samuel Goldwyn (who produced) and William Wyler (who directed) even borrowed the ending of *Smilin' Through* for the film's final image, a long shot of the lovers wandering over their beloved moors, inseparable in death.

It should be mentioned that Emily Brontë, like George du Maurier, has always held a very special appeal for the French Surrealists, who upheld an ideal of love as an absolute, exacerbated passion. When, in 1953, it was announced that Luis Buñuel, once a Surrealist film maker, was about to remake *Wuthering Heights* in Mexico, there was considerable and logical anticipation in film circles. Alas, it turned out to be one of the master's few negligible errors. It was obvious, woodenly acted in the worst soap-opera style, even less passionate than the Goldwyn-Wyler version. Buñuel did, however, preserve that astonishing passage in the book wherein Heathcliff, driven by passion and remorse, attempts to exhume Cathy's body during a stormy night. The lighting, composition and camera set-up irresistibly remind one of a similar moment in that most famous of horror films, *The Bride of Frankenstein*, when The Monster first stumbles (quite literally) across the shrouded remains of the woman who will soon become his mate. Coincidence or conscious homage to the horror film genre? Subject to the vigilance of the Hays and Johnson Codes, American films had to find covert expression for The Unmentionable in such

genres like horror, which would not be taken seriously by censor or critics.

Now and then, a fascination with an idealized past replaced such morbid pursuits, as in *Berkeley Square* ('33), adapted by John L. Balderston from the Henry James novella, 'A Sense of the Past'. The hero in the story, Peter Standish, is obsessed with one of his ancestors who lived in what seems to him to be a more graceful and enlightened era than the drab workaday present of the 30s. In a clap of thunder and some eerie atmospheric detail, which actually covers up the rickety mechanisms of the original play, Standish transports himself to the London of Sir Joshua Reynolds and Mrs Siddons, and also, unfortunately for him, of Bedlam. He falls in love with a cousin, Helen Killigrew, the one person in all London not to be shocked by his uncanny knowledge of things and events to come, nor irritated by his manner of addressing everyone as if they were dead; which of course, they are. It takes some more legerdemain to rescue Standish from the madhouse and restore him to his century and ours. In a small London cemetery he discovers the tomb of his beloved Helen, who never married, in the hope that the mysterious visitor from another time would some day return to her. In a situation that irresistibly brings to mind all kinds of comic anachronisms, Leslie Howard and Heather Angel remain touching and delicate and slightly absurd, engaging our sympathies if not our belief. The picture now appears as a genuine curio, stranded in time like its hero. It is all the more surprising that it was remade in England in 1951, as *The House in the Square* (in America, *I'll Never Forget You*), lavishing Technicolor on its satins and lace, reserving a cerulean monochrome for those

Trilby **(1923). Andrée Lafayette with Arthur Edmond Carew as Svengali. Carew was a well-known specialist in villainous roles.**
Svengali **(1931). John Barrymore and Marian Marsh (as Trilby).**

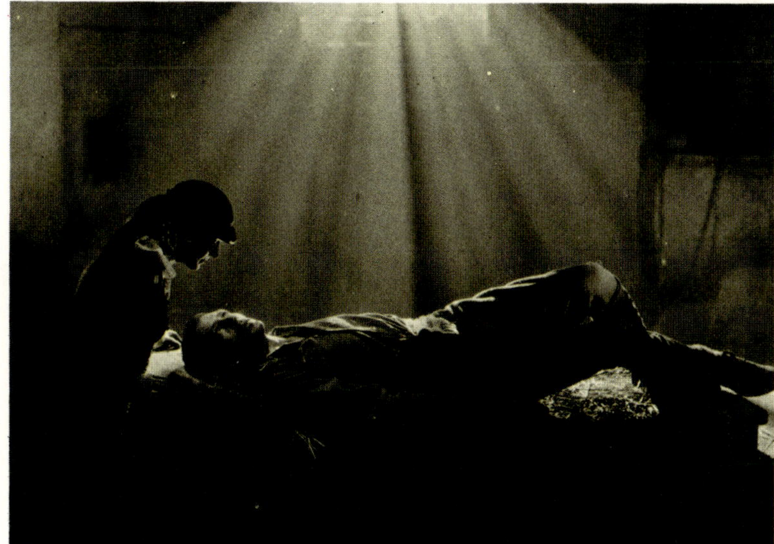

The Duchess of Towers (Ann Harding) comes to the imprisoned Peter (Gary Cooper) in a dream visit. *Peter Ibbetson* **(1935).**

From transcendental rat to Transylvanian demon lover – three versions of *Dracula*: **Max Schreck in** *Nosferatu* **(1923), Bela Lugosi in** *Dracula* **(1931), and Christopher Lee in** *Dracula Has Risen From The Grave* **(1968).**

scenes laid in the twentieth century, and rewarding the lovesick Peter Standish with a modern reincarnation of the late Helen Killigrew, a happy ending as prosaic as the mere mating of mortals is wont to be.

But all of Hollywood's inconsistencies and vagaries, its lack of taste and humour, its tendency to flinch in the face of reality, may be forgiven in the delighted afterglow of such surprises as *The Ghost and Mrs Muir* ('47), *Portrait of Jenny* ('48), and *Pandora and the Flying Dutchman* ('50). For sheer wit and lightness of touch, Joseph L. Mankiewicz never topped *The Ghost and Mrs Muir*. It is a subtle and literate romantic comedy about a pretty young widow. She rents a house on the Cornish coast which is haunted by the ghost of a salty, blustery sea captain who, at first, attempts to scare her away, and failing to do so, settles down to a rich personal relationship. The Captain also dictates his memoirs to Mrs Muir, which in turn become a best-selling book that brings financial security to the widow and her little daughter. There are, however, limits to the friendship; and when a real suitor arrives on the scene to pay court, the Captain bids a passionate adieu to Mrs Muir and departs from her life, without leaving trace of his passage. The widow never re-marries. At her life's end, she discovers the faithful ghost nearby. 'Somehow, I always felt you by my side,' she confides to him in a scene of such ineffable grace that it instantly obliterates any previous memory of similar scenes. The picture playfully upsets the conventions of both the ghost-story and the love-beyond-death romance. Rex Harrison plays the Captain with carnal relish, not as a mere disembodied spirit but as a symbol of freedom and adventure, of the reckless existence denied to the spunky little widow because of her sex. And Gene Tierney, with her haunted face and fragile air, does well by Mrs Muir's ethereal charm and quiet resolve. Unlike many a fantasy, the picture never exorcises the ghost as either dream figure, fantasy or source of inspiration welling up from the deeper recesses of Mrs Muir's being. He remains a ghost, as real as any ghost, but twice as romantic.

Based on a novel by Robert Nathan, *Portrait of Jenny* reverses the situation of *The Ghost and Mrs Muir* by having Adam (Joseph Cotten), a struggling young New York painter, meet one day in Central Park a strange little girl who explains, between sobs, that her parents have been killed in an accident. She then disappears in the same fortuitous manner that she appeared. Later, he runs into her again; she is no longer a child but a budding adolescent whose beauty awakens the artist in Adam. Attempting to capture her elusive qualities on canvas, he notices that she is growing up almost visibly before his eyes. By the time she appears for the third time, Adam is in love with the mysterious Jenny. It is the last time, however, as she is reclaimed by the sea, where she drowned years back and from whence she has miraculously returned to seek the love she never found in life. A mountainous wave sweeps her away, and all that will remain of Adam's romance is his portrait of Jenny which hangs in time at the Metropolitan Museum for all the world to admire and wonder: did she really exist?

Where *Portrait of Jenny* is kept small and intimate, it succeeds quite well. It is not easy to turn Manhattan into an enchanted landscape,

Berkeley Square (1933). Leslie Howard as Peter Standish, Heather Angel as Anne Killigrew.
Widow and ghost strike up a bizarre, touching relationship. Gene Tierney and Rex Harrison in _The Ghost And Mrs Muir_ (1947).

but the director, William Dieterle, does the trick with the assistance of highly artificial Northern lighting, a gallery of picturesque characters and frosty location scenes in Central Park. But somewhere along the production, David O. Selznick lost his confidence in the material and decided to turn the film into a multi-million spectacular. He added music by Debussy (classical, but still spooky), arty shots, photographed through burlap to make them look like paintings, and a climactic storm sequence during which the screen expanded to the size of Cinerama (then, many years away) and acquired a greenish tint. Selznick all but overwhelms the story, but fortunately not his wife, the actress Jennifer Jones, for whose greater glory the project was conceived. She remains ideally cast as a child-woman-ghost, with her luminous eyes and nervous mouth hinting at the brevity of her time on earth, the most memorable thing in the film.

Once in a while along comes a film so bold, so reckless in its mixing of genres and film metaphor, so extravagant in its execution, and so imbued with conviction in its faults as much as its virtues that one cannot help admiring it despite glaring defects or lack of taste. Such a film is *Pandora and the Flying Dutchman,* not only a poetic title but literal as well, a creation of Albert Lewin, an offbeat producer and director also responsible for *The Picture of Dorian Gray. Pandora* contains some of the purplest prose in film history, and some outrageous plotting as well. Pandora is an American playgirl for whom men die willingly: one discarded suitor quietly poisons himself as she playfully sings at the piano: 'How am I to know if it's really love that found its way here?'. She is all set to marry a racing millionaire, when she discovers a white yacht anchored in a small harbour off the Spanish fishing town where she is vacationing with her friends. On impulse, she swims to the yacht that night, and there she meets The Flying Dutchman of myth and opera, who has been sailing the sea for the last four centuries as punishment for murdering his wife, whom he wrongly suspected of infidelity. Pandora falls in love the moment she learns that only a woman's selfless sacrifice can redeem him and set his soul at rest. She sails away with The Dutchman, leaving behind a wake of death and disaster. Her fiancé crashes in his racing car. The Gypsy bullfighter who loves her lets himself be gored in the ring for looking too deep into The Dutchman's fathomless eyes. If all this sounds absurd beyond belief, it *is* absurd. Yet the picture somehow makes it all plausible, as it erects its own system of logic from such disparate elements as Technicolor, exotic locations, surreal touches, jazz and flamenco music. Lewin's flamboyant directions may lack the authority with which Jean Cocteau trod similar ground, but his images are consistently beautiful, and sometimes even a poetic moment is allowed to flash across the screen, even if it is only the kinetic poetry of Ava Gardner's gestures as she emerges from the sea. Smouldering under her marble-cold, classical beauty, Ava laid her claim here to be billed as 'the most beautiful animal in the world'. James Mason, more beetle-browed and gloomy than ever, is a suitably tormented Dutchman. *Pandora* succeeded in its own terms, which is the reason it closes the chapter. It also serves as farewell to supernatural romance, since missing from the screen, but surviving with more effort than success, on television.

The inquisitive Pandora (Ava Gardner) and the immortal Flying Dutchman (James Mason) meet in Albert Levin's *Pandora And The Flying Dutchman* **(1951).**

CHAPTER FOUR

'There once was a land of Cavaliers and Cotton Fields
called the Old South . . .
Here in this pretty world Gallantry took its last bow . . .
Here was the last ever to be seen of Knights
and their Ladies Fair, of Master and of Slave . . .
Look for it only in books,
for it is no more than a dream remembered.'

Prologue for GONE WITH THE WIND

SOURCES OF ROMANCE

Theatre-goers had Julia Marlowe; movie-goers had The Vitagraph Girl, a democratic beauty who boldly stepped into Miss Marlowe's slippers to play Juliet in 1908 with no experience other than a childhood in vaudeville as Baby Flo, The Child Wonder Whistler. As a matter of fact, she didn't even have a name, Vitagraph refusing to identify the players in their product. Belasco and Frohman and all the other great Broadway producers must have smiled with condescension at first, then wondered.

For no legitimate impresario on Broadway or the West End had ever offered Shakespeare for a nickel, and anyway, the classes that patronized Nickelodeons and early movie parlours would not have paid a nickel to see Shakespeare performed on stage. Theatre was not their turf, but movies belonged to them.

The motion picture now offered them much more than the world of Edison and the Lumière brothers; it had quickly taken hold of every other form of spectacle, from pantomime, circus, ballet and religious pageant to puppet shows (which 'flickers' resembled greatly) to the more sophisticated forms of opera and drama.

Drama had caught the eye of the camera; but it was an eye out of sympathy in a medium devoid of sound, exposing every line in the face and every crack in the plaster, distorting movement into jerky spasms, reducing the most complex dramatic structure to any two or three basic situations, and releasing the mangled, voiceless film adaptations of celebrated classics to the distributors at 12 cents a foot.

Stars were to bridge the awful gap between romance and the movies. Flattened out across the screen, reduced to silence and robbed of complexion, they still managed to breathe life into their roles. The better-known performers usually brought their most popular stage roles with them, even when they knew that the film was hardly equipped to do them justice. But the names of these classics were enough to bring the public to the movie houses in search of high-class entertainment.

The cinema tradition of romance stems from these high-flown and slightly frayed costume dramas, as well as from opera, Biblical stories and even history. Not many books could manage a direct transition to the screen without the help of an intermediate stage or opera version. It took the charisma of the matinée idol or of the leading lady to put them over. Then, gradually, the cinema sifted cinematic wheat from theatrical chaff, discarding performers whatever their reputation on the stage. The grand manner had to go; the camera was too big for those gestures. Popular as some of these classic adaptations were, in reality they slowed down the march of progress.

It was to take years to shed the theatrical manner, but by the time Geraldine Farrar left the Metropolitan Opera House to do *Carmen* for Cecil B. De Mille a mere three years later, the medium had learned a thing or two, one being that the best way to deal with a prima donna was to rub her into the dirt. Farrar was more mischievous and also more daring than one had a right to expect. She bares her teeth and swings her hips with all the reckless abandon demanded by Mr De Mille. She was the best Carmen the movies had seen until then, and that included Theda Bara whose version was released simultaneously.

After the First War, romance really began to flourish, but in a

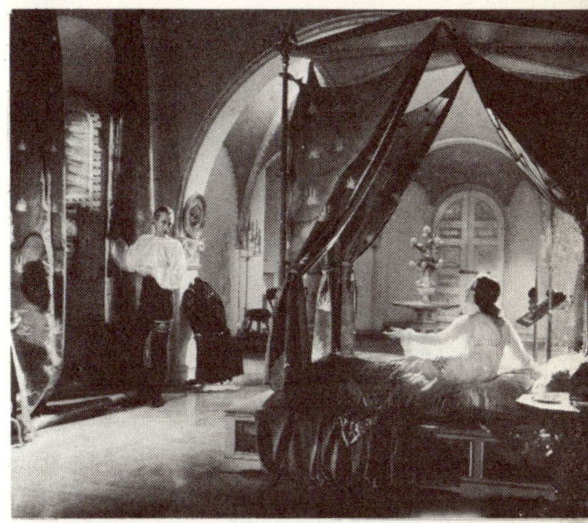

With *Hamlet*, *Romeo And Juliet* remains the most screened of Shakespeare's plays, having been made into more than 20 films. In 1916, Theda Bara and Harry Hilliard were the over-age lovers. In 1936 it was Leslie Howard and Norma Shearer. In 1953, the much younger Laurence Harvey and Susan Shentall.

Romeo And Juliet **(1968). The youngest star-crossed lovers ever, Leonard Whiting and Olivia Hussey. A modern-dress musical version of** *Romeo And Juliet:* *West Side Story* **(1961) starred Natalie Wood and Richard Beymer.**

quite unexpected manner. Partly because of the ever-present thirst for escapism, partly because Americans had been 'over there' and discovered wicked old Europe, romance became all of a sudden a foreign commodity. No longer could one have a heroine named Mary or a hero named John. Now it was Carmelita, Gerda or Bella Donna (all incarnations of Pola Negri), or Julio, Alonzo and Ahmed Ben Hassan (all played by Valentino). Even Douglas Fairbanks renounced his Americanness to become D'Artagnan, Zorro, Don Q or The Gaucho, or The Thief of Baghdad.

With the 20s dawned the Era of Wonderful Nonsense, the heyday of romance as imagined and set forth by Vicente Blasco Ibanez and Elinor Glyn, an unlikely couple who gave the decade a couple of archetypal images to rival those of The Flapper, The Gangster and The Lounge Lizard. Ibanez was a man of the world with a first-hand knowledge of Paris and Monte Carlo, the desert and the pampas, locations exotic enough for the film-goers of Oshkosh and Walla-Walla. He willed Hollywood a Spain of picturesque locales and fundamental passions. To the movies, Spain meant two things: bullfights and passion. Argentina, on the other hand, stood for passion and tango, as in *The Four Horsemen of the Apocalypse*. And the War, which interfered with the love affair, brought on another Ibanez legacy, the tragic ending. Somehow, someone had to pay for all that passion. Freya, the spy in *Mare Nostrum* ('26), dies before a firing squad while her lover, Ferragut, sinks with his ship. (For the tender-hearted, however, there was a haunting epilogue in which Freya and Ferragut were

Carmen has driven Don José to murder in more than 20 films. In 1942, Viviane Romance and Jean Marais essayed the roles in a French version. In 1948, it was Rita Hayworth and Glenn Ford. In the most effective switch to

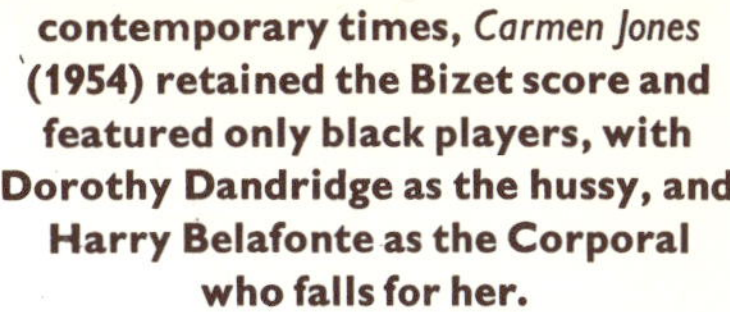
contemporary times, *Carmen Jones* (1954) retained the Bizet score and featured only black players, with Dorothy Dandridge as the hussy, and Harry Belafonte as the Corporal who falls for her.

reunited in the deep.) Today, one can safely laugh off Ibanez and his pretentious pacifism: war was hell, but it was also highly cinematic.

Madame Glyn, however, offered the public tiger skins and beds of roses, etiquette and Ruritanian kingdoms. (Ibanez at least named his no less mythical countries after the real thing.) At best, the plot in her adaptations was an excuse to elaborate sexual tension, which was finally dissipated in the last reel; though not through seduction or rape, since no heroine was ever dishonoured in a Glyn movie, and no man was ever a brute at heart.

It must be said that La Glyn managed to transmit her own nostalgia for the vanished manners of the Edwardian era to millions of American picture-goers who had never heard of Edward VII and drank tea only when they had a cold. Madame was also an authority on the universal subject of love. Her theories and reflections were collected and published in 1924 under the title of 'The Philosophy of Love', and it contained helpful chapters on 'How to ignite love' and 'Things that make a woman cheap or common'. It was probably her only book never to be made into a movie. Having scored with *Beyond the Rocks, Three Weeks, The Only Thing* and *Love's Blindness* – peopled with the usual aristocrats in the usual sumptuous settings – she did a most remarkable, and fortunate, about-face in discovering that Clara Bow had It, that indefinable *je ne sais quoi* which Aileen Pringle, Pauline Starke and Eleanor Boardman lacked despite their tiaras and their manners, and which Bow dispensed so generously with a wink and a wiggle.

It would be nice to think that Bow brought it all back home single-handed, but what really sounded the knell on Ibanez, Glyn and their followers was sound itself. The moment one could hear those lines out loud one ceased to be charmed. Gilbert's voice was not half as ridiculous as the lines he had to mouth in his talkie debut. Lines were often ridiculous in the silent movies, but certain things are better left unheard. De Mille's silent *The Ten Commandments* offered some prize dialogue titles: Nita Naldi vamps Rod La Rocque: 'Come for lunch and I'll give you Nyr-gar-pay, a liquor distilled from a thousand lotus flowers.' After he shoots her, she seethes: 'Goodbye, Danny dear . . . I'll tell the Devil you're not far behind.' Try to imagine anyone speaking the lines without choking. Silence was golden in many ways, not least because it preserved the unreality of these movie worlds. Sound is still the most lifelike thing about a movie.

But the memory of success dies hard; what had served once could be put back into service, this time with words and music restored. The 30s brought enormous conviction, and a kind of finality, to such tired warhorses as *Camille, The Prisoner of Zenda, If I Were King, A Tale of Two Cities*, and *The Count of Monte Cristo*, all of which had known previous incarnations as plays, novels and silent films.

In times of crisis, romance becomes a material necessity. The 30s, as Anthony Shaffer wittily reminds us in his play *Sleuth*, were a time when every Prime Minister had a thriller by his bedside. During the Depression, every American film-goer had Errol Flynn, Ronald Colman and Gary Cooper in period costume; even the embodiment of American pluck, Clark Gable, donned breeches and pigtail to play

Henry James described *Camille* as 'champagne and tears', a potent mixture to judge from the 15-odd film versions to date. Among those that played the role were Nazimova (with Valentino in 1920), Norma Talmadge (with Gilbert Roland in 1927), Micheline Presle in 1952, and Danielle Gaubert in a modern-day adaptation, *Camille 2000* (1968). Best of all, including Bernhardt and Theda Bara, was Garbo, with Robert Taylor as Armand (1936).

Mr Christian in *Mutiny on the Bounty*. This side of the ocean, an Elizabethan swashbuckler, *Fire over England*, served as a discreet reminder that Britain too could fight. And *The Scarlet Pimpernel* kept his aristocratic cool in the shadow of Madame Guillotine.

These were less adaptations from the classics than *classic* adaptations from the juvenile shelf, with something for everyone: action for the kiddies, production values for their elders, and even one or two flashes of the real thing for the more demanding. The genre developed its own ritualistic confrontation between hero and villain, offering a thin veneer of historical authenticity and a reassuring optimism. It also offered a variety of highly florid, but effective dialogue. From *Captain Blood*:

> 'I'm a thief and a pirate and I'll show you how a pirate can deal. Once you bought me for ten measly pounds; now I've bought you for considerably more. Now I own you: you're mine to do with as I please.'

Was this an improvement on the worlds dreamed by Ibanez and Glyn? Times could not have changed that much in a decade, but the movies had. The swashbucklers appealed to the adolescent in everyone.

Of course, the previous generation had had their Captain Blood and their Robin Hood and their Prisoner of Zenda, and each era has its own way of interpreting things. But already in the 30s (let alone in the 70s) Fairbanks *et al.* looked much too middle-aged, and their

leading ladies much too dowdy, when compared with the new stars, Errol Flynn and Olivia de Havilland. The first *Robin Hood* had fantasy castles and staggering spectacle overshadowing Fairbanks's own considerable charm. But there has not been a Robin Hood worth remembering since Errol Flynn took over the green tights and feathered cap, just as there has been no Camille since Garbo, or other Villon after Colman.

The rightness of it all was underlined by the plush romantic scores of Korngold, Steiner and Newman which swept the viewer away along with the action. These composers found their inspiration in the classical works of Ravel, Stravinsky and Richard Strauss, but were working mostly in the romantic mode as if taking their cues from the films themselves.

THE WORLD OF ELINOR GLYN
John Gilbert and Aileen Pringle in *His Hour* **(1923).**
Eleanor Boardman as Queen Thyra and Conrad Nagel as The Duke in *The Only Thing* **(1925).**
Aileen Pringle and Conrad Nagel *Three Weeks* **(1924). In Venice – the last night of happiness before the separation.**

The cloak-and-sword vogue extended as well to historical films, where not surprisingly the accent remained on affairs of the heart rather than those of state, but with the action played down and the pageantry emphasized. As usual, the cinema was following the stage, where Maxwell Anderson's chronicles of Mary Stuart and Elizabeth the First were holding sway. The public, however, kept expecting Errol Flynn to unleash his sword and run through those scheming courtiers bent on breaking up his love affair with Bette Davis, in *The Private Lives of Elizabeth and Essex* ('39). Instead, she sends him to his death in the Tower of London. Gone was the happy insouciance of worlds well lost for love. Historical movies could afford the luxury of a few political issues; but, make no mistake about it, history had always to be explained in terms of romance.

A few years earlier, Stroheim had relished cutting the Hapsburgs down to size, and Lubitsch had cast his monarchs as bumbling shopkeepers, their consorts as saucy soubrettes with an eye for the nearest hussar. But around the mid-30s, Hollywood turned passionately royalist. Katherine Hepburn's *Mary of Scotland* ('36) mounted the scaffold as the innocent scapegoat of Scottish intransigence and Elizabethan jealousy. Carlotta of Mexico (Bette Davis again) went insane after the execution of her husband Maximilian, in *Juarez* ('39). The whole of Europe held its breath and waited while Napoleon (Charles Boyer) and Maria Walewska (Garbo) went through a minuet, in *Conquest* ('37). In England, Anna Neagle fluttered and flounced as Victoria in two films that fell on the duller side of hagiography. James Agate saluted her as 'Victoria The Little'. Whatever Hollywood's faults, queens and kings were super-stars, and vice-versa.

The picture that sums up the trend is not Garbo's *Queen Christina* which seems to have set the pattern, but Norma Shearer's *Marie Antoinette* ('38). In Shearer's alabaster hands, the arrogant, obtuse spendthrift of history (and Stefan Zweig's biography which the studio had acquired) became 'Toinette, 'the tragic doll of Le Trianon', to quote one of 'Photoplay's' transports. But where Garbo's film was relatively modest, the Shearer vehicle enjoyed a munificence rare even for Hollywood, bestowed on it by Sun King Louis B. Mayer. Shearer's Marie Antoinette, emotional and ladylike, is provided with a series of alibis to justify her later reckless extravagance; she is disappointed in her marriage by her husband's impotence; but worse, she

DAMSEL AND KNIGHT
Errol Flynn and Olivia de Havilland in *Captain Blood* (1935), and in *The Adventures Of Robin Hood* (1937). Ronald Colman as the poet-rogue Francois Villon, and Francis Dee as Princess Katharine in *If I Were King* (1938).

is snubbed by Madame Dubarry, favourite of the reigning Louis XV. Marie Antoinette gets her revenge when the old king dies and her husband ascends the throne; she packs Dubarry out of Versailles. She then meets her true love, Count Fersen (Tyrone Power by way of Madame Tussaud) who is at first appalled at the lady's frivolity. There are obligatory *malentendus* before they are holding moonlit trysts in the gardens of Versailles, despite the fact that history and Zweig refused to authenticate the romance. The major irony of the film is that, having made mincemeat out of fact, it becomes most effective when adhering closely to it. Once dethroned, widowed, and robbed of her children and her pride, Shearer and the character grow in stature. One should forgive the final *coup de theatre* because it works to perfection, and allows Shearer her finest hour. Looking like David's merciless sketch of the queen on the tumbril, Shearer's eyes fill with tears as a double exposure gives us in heartbreaking contrast the starry-eyed young princess of the film's early reels, on her first step to the throne and tragedy: 'Think of it, Maman, I shall be Queen . . . Queen of France.'

The one Hollywood film of the period that did not conform either to history or the standard romantic treatment was *The Scarlet Empress* ('34), which followed the baroque inspiration of its director, Josef von Sternberg, and portrayed Catherine of Russia with the timeless features of Marlene Dietrich, ruthless as Richard the Third and exquisite as an icon. The same year as Sternberg's masterpiece flopped, another much tamer version of the same character appeared in a British production from the Korda studios, with Elizabeth Bergner playing a pussy cat where Dietrich had been a tigress. Both versions sank without a trace at the time; but the Sternberg film was rediscovered, first by Eisenstein, whose operatic, grandiose *Ivan the Terrible* seemed to echo the delirious ornateness of its predecessor, and finally by the public of the 60s, less romantic than those of the 30s, and thus more appreciative of Sternberg's achievement.

Today's viewpoint has radically shifted to the side of demystification, crowned heads of the past being exposed as petty, boring little men and women, from whom one can draw a contemporary parallel and read the fate of nations in their exposed dirty linen.

Historians have been known to differ, and films have always capitalized on the ambiguity of historical characters. Thus, we have had *They Died with Their Boots On* pitted against *Custer of the West* (not forgetting the deadly cartoon of Custer in *Little Big Man*); two conflicting versions of *The Charge of the Light Brigade*; Henry VIII as charming scoundrel and as heartless despot; Elizabeth I as ruthless empire builder and as a lonely woman with a penchant for younger, and prettier, men. Every generation delights in exposing the clay feet of established idols and perhaps, had Hollywood not been so overtly romantic in the 30s and 40s, this would be a less sceptical period.

Halfway between history and cloak-and-sword romance, there developed that uniquely American mixture of piety and prurience, of old-time tent revival and kooch dance, the Biblical epic. Of the latter-day scholars – expert at refashioning and reinterpreting the Scriptures – the most successful is still Cecil B. De Mille, although

Norma Shearer in the historical extravaganza, *Marie Antoinette* **(1938).**

Parquet floors, imperial eagles, waltzes and Ruritania. Stewart Granger and Deborah Kerr in the 1952 version of Anthony Hope's evergreen *The Prisoner Of Zenda*.

Sexual politics: Catherine The Great (Marlene Dietrich) usurps the throne of Russia in *The Scarlet Empress* **(1934).**

in fact merely four of his films were actually based on the Good Book itself. Nor was De Mille the inventor of the genre, that honour like most of the others going instead to Griffith, whose *Judith of Bethulia* ('13) was a shrewd combination of Apocrypha and Carny Show, and even depicted a very desirable Judith (Blanche Sweet) indulging in a sympathetic flirtation with Holophernes (Henry B. Walthall) before getting him drunk and cutting off his head.

De Mille came to the Bible in easy gradual steps. He delighted in having his contemporary comedies flash occasionally back into the past, which allowed him to indulge his penchant for mass scenes, grandiose sets and bizarre costumes. Such flashbacks occur, for example, in the very bright and modern *Male and Female* ('19) wherein the admirable Crichton (Thomas Meigham) daydreams of himself as a barbaric king humiliating a captive princess (Swanson). In *Manslaughter* ('22) the puritanical hero (Meigham again) fantasized himself as the barbaric conqueror out to break the spirit of a haughty Roman lady. It was obvious that a covert sado-masochism was one of the main forces behind De Mille and his heroes. In *The Ten Commandments* ('23), the flashback has become a longer prologue to the modern story, conceived in a truly grandiose scale but still somewhat like static *tableaux* despite desert locations and hundreds of extras. *The King of Kings* ('27) could not stray from the New Testament for obvious reasons, maintaining a Sunday School reverence where the Christ figure (played by H. B. Warner) was concerned, but at last letting go with Mary Magdalene (Jacqueline Logan) who made her

Cleopatra* (1934), directed by Cecil B. de Mille, boasts of an extravagant seduction scene. Cleopatra (Claudette Colbert) and Mark Antony (Henry Wilcoxon) in the royal galley which turns into a sensuous floor show.

Early Biblical story: D. W. Griffith's *Judith Of Bethulia* (1913) with Blanche Sweet as the Jewish widow and Henry B. Walthall as Holophernes, soon to lose his head.

entrance in a chariot drawn by zebras and was attended by scores of Nubian slaves, a far cry from the humble sinner of Magdala.

You will not find *The Sign of the Cross* ('32) in the Acts of the Apostles, and *Cleopatra* ('34) remains totally vernacular, despite the presence of a Biblical transfuge, Herod Antiphas, as a major character.

Having only history to contend with, De Mille can indulge all his fantasies. His Cleopatra rolls out of a carpet blessed with the modern allure and husky laughter of Claudette Colbert, to take her place on the screen without benefit of Shakespearean poetry or Shavian debate. De Mille had learned an important lesson, that characters had to be rendered in contemporary terms, like super stars.

Critics, then as now hung up on words, were blind to his bold, suggestive imagery. There was more than spectacle in De Mille's pictures: in *Samson and Delilah* ('49), he had the temptress redeem herself at the end and share the fate of her blind victim by leading Samson to the columns that support the temple of the Philistines. Cannily, De Mille has Victor Mature lit and made up to suggest a Christ figure, only it is a Christ who has known and succumbed to temptation. While Hedy Lamarr, in dark hood and cape, becomes the archetypal Pieta in brutal contrast to the sinuous siren of the rest of the film. At his best, De Mille was a master at juxtaposing such symbols, and he backed his Biblical epics with the faith of the fundamentalist.

Joan Fontaine in *Frenchman's Creek* (1944); Fontaine again in *Rebecca* (1940); Olivia de Havilland and Richard Burton in *My Cousin Rachel* (1953), all drawn from novels by Daphne du Maurier.

In old and certainly sexist times, a woman's picture was a disparaging label attached by critics, predominantly male, to certain films geared to the greater enjoyment of the female audience, and which were no more damnable in themselves than such celebrations of male brawn and prowess as the western and the war drama. Today, the most common accusation hurled at these films – that men in them were so much expendable cardboard – has ironically rebounded in the opposite direction, for women are slowly but surely vanishing from the contemporary American film. One has but to look at *The Last Detail, Midnight Cowboy, Butch Cassidy and the Sundance Kid* or even *The Godfather* to realize that they all dispense with women except as so much set decoration.

The world in a woman's picture was conceived as woman's battlefield. The point of view was exclusively female. The man was usually riding out to war or in search of fame and fortune, while the woman stayed behind to raise the children, and if she was an Edna Ferber heroine, to build empires. Ferber was the best-loved American writer in the 20s and 30s, and although her gifts could not compare with those of Eudora Welty or Willa Cather, she was head and shoulders above other practitioners of the genre such as Fannie Hurst, Faith Baldwin, Ursula Parrott and Kathleen Norris. The Ferber novels possessed a grand, fresh-air sweep, a pioneer robustness; they spanned several generations and served as journalistic reportage on the growing, expanding United States. The Ferber heroine witnessed the passing of the proud river boats, the evolution of the theatre, and the loss of tradition, as with Magnolia in *Show Boat*. If she was Sabra Cravat, heroine of the hugely popular *Cimarron*, she steered the wild

Oklahoma territory into statehood. As Selina Peake in *So Big*, she could look back on a lifetime of devotion and sacrifice, knowing herself to be the maker of great men, and the moving force behind change and progress. The Ferber heroine could mourn a lost love, a dead husband or a son gone astray without impairing the final uplifting effect, since they seemed to be, like Eleonora Duse, comfortable in tragedy. Theirs was a life of achievement, and they held it as a shining example to millions of readers and film-goers.

The movies did very well by Miss Ferber, making and remaking the novels into preordained successes. *Cimarron* was filmed twice, *So Big* three times, and *Show Boat*, with the added enchantment of one of Jerome Kern's best scores, became a classic and was also filmed three times. Lesser novels like *Come and Get It* and *Saratoga Trunk* made even better movies. When working for the stage, Miss Ferber chose to temper her own sentimental vein with the acid wit of George S. Kaufman: there is not one sentimental mother-love play among the lot.

Fannie Hurst ran Ferber a close second, but they were poles apart, although both had the long-suffering American woman as heroine. Hurst's leading ladies had to contend with their own racial backgrounds, not to mention those added by the melting pot; their background was decidedly urban, their problems and conflict arising from either prejudice or established morality.

It should be noted here that women novelists had displaced their male competitors by the mid-30s as a steady source for film adaptations. In the silent era, especially before 1920, the most oft-filmed author had been Jack London, with Mark Twain and Joseph Hergesheimer chalking up numerous film adaptations. But with the early sound success of *Cimarron* in 1931, of *Imitation of Life* in 1934, of *Rebecca* in 1940, the future of the woman's picture and that of the woman novelist was consolidated. So much so that men too began to dabble in the genre. James Hilton, author of *Lost Horizon* and *Goodbye, Mr Chips* (which are essentially male stories), wrote what is probably the ideal woman's picture, *Random Harvest*, filmed in 1942; and Louis Bromfield wrote *The Life of Vergie Winters* before *The Rains Came*, and in the early 40s a dynastic novel in the Ferber manner, *Mrs Parkington*. Hollywood kept an eye on the best-selling list, constantly delving into contemporary American literature, and actually neglecting the classics. Jack London, Twain and Dreiser virtually disappeared from the screen, which was taken over either by the newer talents or by European imports like A. J. Cronin, Daphne Du Maurier, Erich Maria Remarque and Vicki Baum, all household names to the movie-going public.

From Daphne Du Maurier, they learned to expect a Cornish landscape of sea, rock and wind-lashed manor houses, a touch of the macabre and a very well-wrought romantic intrigue. Her novels had a period of their own and were filled with echoes of Henry James and Charlotte Brontë. She had an unmatched talent for opening lines. 'Last night I dreamt I went to Manderley again' says the nameless heroine of *Rebecca*, and although Europe was darkening and America felt uncertain and unstable, Manderley filled everybody's dreams, a

In the Biblical non-epic, *David And Bathsheba* (1951), Gregory Peck and Susan Hayward portrayed the guilty tormented lovers of antiquity.

Samson as Christ figure, Delilah as Madonna. Victor Mature and Hedy Lamarr in De Mille's *Samson And Delilah* (1949).

mixture of fairy castle and haunted house, reeking of beautiful Rebecca's perfume and echoing with her footsteps. The original, no mean achievement in its own genre, was actually improved by Alfred Hitchcock, who made his first American film from it; but Miss Du Maurier also contributed to change the director's style from the jerky, mechanical succession of 'strong' moments of his British pictures, to a velvet-soft, atmospheric fluidity. Miss Du Maurier also provided the subject for Hitchcock's last British picture, *Jamaica Inn* ('39), and years later was to serve him well with a short story, *The Birds.*

Anna Sten starred in the watered-down Hollywood version of Zola's novel *Nana* (1934).

Vivien Leigh in the British remake of 1948 followed in Garbo's footsteps as Tolstoy's heroine, *Anna Karenina*.

Repetition dulls experience, and most of Miss Du Maurier's novels were so widely imitated – i.e. *Dragonwick, Ivy, Lightning Strikes Twice* – that by 1952, *My Cousin Rachel* which was the formula as before, did not create a ripple other than that provided by Richard Burton in his American debut.

The most read novel of the period, and the most successful film until the advent of *The Godfather*, was, of course, *Gone With the Wind*, the work of a Southern writer who was never to publish again, Margaret Mitchell. Her saga of the passing of the Old South, part wistful recollection, part historical primer, had for a centre a heroine worthy of a practised novelist, a first-rate bitch-girl, indomitable, amoral, unfulfilled. Six directors, a legion of writers and all the technique that money could buy were put at the disposal of the film. In a superb swirl of spectacle, the audience could forget that Scarlett O'Hara was left without husband, child, would-be-lover or a friend in the world, save for faithful old Mammy. The picture's ultimate triumph was that, despite its inordinate running time and a heroine that stubbornly refused to grow, one could not find it in oneself to answer her 'But, what will I do? Where will I go?' with Rhett Butler's resigned, indifferent 'Frankly, my dear, I don't give a damn.' In *Gone With the Wind*, romance is everywhere except in the heroine's heart, which makes it a masterpiece *manqué.*

Romance does not imply lack of depth, as is often charged, but very conscious imagery and stylization, a careful deletion of every element not conforming to a romantic pattern. Its conventions must be instantly recognized by the viewer, the attitudes of a character rendered in sharp, unambiguous lines. It will not do, for instance, to make Karenin too sympathetic, or Nana too coldly calculating. In the terms of the romantic film, the former stands for the Cruel School Master who lays down the law for the heroine, the latter for Retribution and the Redeeming Power of Love. This is partly the after-effect of compressing the World's Best Books in one hundred minutes of screen time; partly a supercilious belief on the part of the film producers that the average movie-goer has not read either Tolstoy or Zola, although both authors have been favourites for decades. In a more formal sense, this sort of visual short-hand is a time-saving device.

The trouble with *Anna Karenina* or *Madame Bovary*, to cite but two of the most ambitious adaptations, is that the boundaries are too wide; to succeed at all, the adaptors must isolate one single strand from a very rich pattern. Usually, the strand selected from the classic

Audrey Hepburn in King Vidor's version of Tolstoy's *War And Peace*. (1955).

is a romantic one. Hollywood's Emma Bovary is a distant cousin to Flaubert's; to most people, the bare outlines of *Anna Karenina* and *Madame Bovary* suggests a poignant romanticism which the reading of the books will not support. On the page, Anna is not the highly romanticized image Garbo made of her, but to have done justice to the original would have been to make another sort of film. Instead of Tolstoy's Anna Karenina, it was Garbo's. An actress like Garbo or Jennifer Jones, given a chance to play Anna or Emma Bovary, even when the script has reduced the original to formula, will still appear on the screen carrying with her the original character she has absorbed; and the camera will pick it up. No matter how watered down the original, they convey through their personal understanding all the elements left out in the adaptation.

A shrewd expressive director like Vincente Minnelli approaches the adaptation of *Madame Bovary* with the original in mind, and still makes it work on both levels, of romance and denunciation of romance. The film is faithful to Flaubert in the final pricking of the romantic balloon, after letting it soar for most of the film. Very few moments in romantic cinema match Emma's whirling waltz, the smashing of the windows with the furniture, the exquisite shot of Emma beholding herself in a gilt mirror, the very image of her dreams. The images gradually become more sober; Emma's romantic delusions will finally do her in. It may not be totally Flaubert, and neither was Renoir's equally successful although less free adaptation. It is an American reading of Flaubert, a very skilful translation of themes, ideas and attitudes to the Hollywood idiom, and it is less a betrayal of the original than a shortening of the inevitable distance between past and present, between the old and new worlds, between media.

Three versions of *Madame Bovary*: From France with Valentine Tessier, one German (1937) with Pola Negri and Ferdinand Marian, and Hollywood's with Jennifer Jones and Louis Jourdan (1949).

CHAPTER FIVE

SOME DIRECTORS

'The more I ponder on the problems of the artist, the less they resemble the problems of the actor.'
Josef von Sternberg

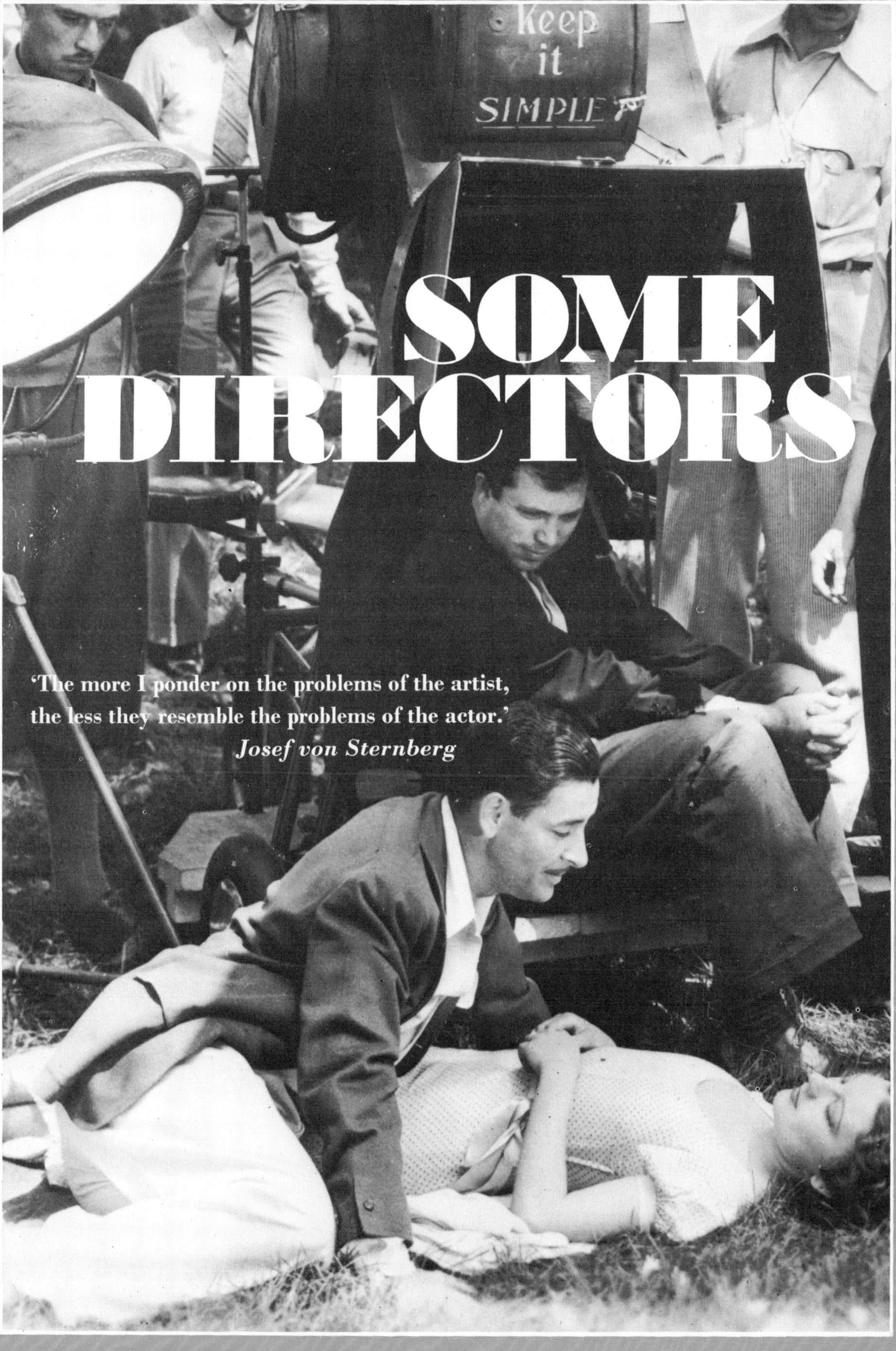

A caption on the screen announces 'It's a tale of temple bells sounding at sunset before the image of Buddha. It is a tale of love and lovers. It is a tale of tears.' The picture, of course, is D. W. Griffith's 1920 masterpiece, *Broken Blossoms*, starring Lillian Gish. Due to the technical developments and stylistic devices pioneered by the film it is scarcely dated by the passage of time. Only its silence reminds us of its era; it is a memorable film; a chamberwork of terror and beauty.

Griffith and Lillian Gish appeared to share a preference for stories of cruelty, terror, prejudice and death. And yet there was beauty in all this grimness. Griffith can do close-ups of feelings, of atmosphere, the way lesser directors do close-ups of faces.

Poetry *was* the human face for Griffith. Lillian Gish could never approach in sound what she conveyed with her silence: her pantomime is so subtle, refined and true.

Griffith's concept of romance rests squarely on his choice of heroines. He had had years in which to perfect Miss Gish's image of besieged innocence, although most of his silent films appear to be moral tales, compact little thrillers, or all-out action stories. Even in *Birth of a Nation* and *Intolerance*, spectacle and drama outweigh the romantic interludes. But already in *Broken Blossoms*, the tension *is* romantic. And *True Heart Susie* concerns itself exclusively with affairs of the heart, having both tenderness and beauty.

Mae Marsh, another of Griffith's heroines, was more piquant than Lillian Gish, but lacked her uncanny gift for understatement: Marsh flutters and flounces too often and too much.

Perhaps Griffith's idea of romance materialized in the person of Carol Dempster, who appeared in eight of his films, most notably in *Isn't Life Wonderful?* Dempster never appeared under any other director and could really run the gamut from waif to flirt (from *The White Rose* to *That Royle Girl*) displaying in *Sally of the Sawdust* a very touching comic gift. With her pinched, spinsterish features, she was still able to convey a certain degree of female maturity and awareness of her own powers.

Griffith's later efforts are much warmer than one has been led to believe by Rotha, Jacobs *et al*. There is nothing new in either *Drums of Love* ('27) or *Lady of the Pavements* ('29), except that in the latter, perhaps for the first time in a Griffith film, the women were portrayed as very desirable and physical.

Griffith had found film an inchoate medium in 1908 and turned it into a potent instrument of communication, establishing conventions and genres that were to be developed by hundreds of American directors in his wake.

D. W. GRIFFITH
Lupe Velez curtsies before her mentor, Jetta Goudal, in Griffith's *Lady Of The Pavements* (1929) which shares its source with Bresson's *Les Dames du Bois de Boulogne*.
In 1924 Griffith made his German film *Isn't Life Wonderful?* in which the valiant young lovers were played by Neil Hamilton and Carol Dempster.

If, like Croce, we are to believe that romanticism is feeling and classicism is representation, then most of Hollywood's great directors deserve to be called classic; only Frank Borzage is entitled to be the great romantic of the American cinema. Borzage entered films as an actor in 1912 and directed for the first time in 1916 (by that time, Griffith had several masterpieces to his credit). He became a consummate technician of the least obtrusive kind, with no particular affection for sustained takes or dramatic editing, just bits and pieces of

Lillian Gish as The Waif in ***Broken Blossoms*** **(1919).**

Massive sets and intimate moments: Elmer Clifton and Constance Talmadge in ***Intolerance*** **(1916).**

Griffith romance: an unmarried mother rescued from the ice floes by the young farmer who knows she is free of guilt. Richard Barthlemess and Lillian Gish in ***Way Down East*** **(1921).**

Neil Hamilton and Carol Dempster in ***The White Rose*** **(1923).**

film strung together and illumined by his intense rapport with the performers. Borzage moved from studio to studio, from the grand Germanic sets at Fox to humble Poverty Row studios like Columbia and Republic working with an assortment of cameramen, writers and performers. Like Vidor he remained a master of the 'one possible set-up', the instinctively right angle for each scene; but everywhere he worked he brought his personal handling of character and relationship.

His career spanned forty-odd years, and his pictures copped the first Gold Medal awarded by Photoplay Magazine, and also the first Academy Award. His first sixteen films are either lost or misplaced. His seventeenth is a highlight of the silent era, an adaptation of the Fannie Hurst novel *Humoresque* ('20) which could have been swamped in racial populism but which came off crisp and well observed.

Borzage was suddenly in great demand. Norma Talmadge, she of the exquisitely perplexed expression, engaged him to guide her in three consecutive pictures, one of which was *Secrets* ('24). In 1925, Borzage directed a masterpiece of Americana, *Lazybones*, with the favourite theme of American writers – the loss of American innocence.

Then, in 1927, *Seventh Heaven*, adapted from a not-too-successful play, propelled Borzage and his stars to the top. Janet Gaynor's Diane was a direct descendant of The Child in *Broken Blossom*, put-upon and terrified.

The greatest romanticist of them all: FRANK BORZAGE.

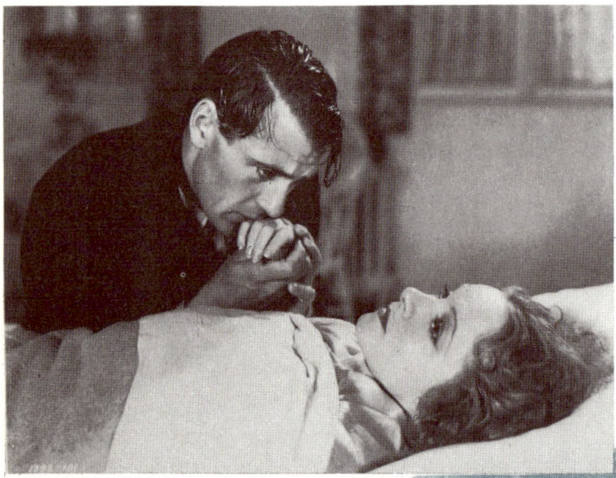

Chico and Diane – Charles Farrell and Janet Gaynor in *Seventh Heaven* **(1927).**
Gary Cooper and Helen Hayes in his adaptation of Hemingway's *A Farewell To Arms* **(1932).**
Clark Gable with Joan Crawford in *Strange Cargo* **(1940).**

After successfully working with Gaynor and Farrell in the bold, operatic *Street Angel*, Borzage changed the mood for *The River* ('28), a slow, sensuous story of a city-weary woman (Mary Duncan in an extraordinary physical part) and a barge-boy (Farrell) stranded in an abandoned river camp during the long months of Northwest winter.

The 30s changed Borzage's outlook. The highly popular Farrell-Gaynor series had seemed to be set in a Never-neverland suited to the sensibilities of the 20s and the technical limitations of the late silent era. With the wolf at the door, audiences grew more resilient, and the movies could allow themselves a bit of social realism. Borzage rose to the occasion with the fine *Man's Castle* ('33) and the touching German idyll, *Little Man What Now?* ('34). His adaptation of Hemingway's *A Farewell to Arms* ('33) dispensed with the rougher edges and covert misogyny of the original. Borzage did not really need the backing of a 'big' author like Hemingway then, and Remarque later; from both, he distilled the same story, that of lovers extracting a few moments of happiness in the face of disaster, exercises in the strength and precariousness of love. He was even better when less hemmed in by significance or prestige as with *Man's Castle* which is done in true Hollywood terms.

Strange how very few proletarian romances were made in the decade. Instead, comedy became madder and madder as it moved into the best social circles; the Crawford stories unrolled in white *moderne* sets, Astaire and Rogers tapped on the dance-floor of our dreams. Romance became a matter of carefree adults in dinner clothes and furs, cruising back and forth the Atlantic. The two romantic highlights of the period are both set on ships, McCarey's *Love Affair* ('38) and Borzage's *History is Made at Night*.

History is Made at Night is the peak of Borzage's experience, exact and economically conceived, moving between situations which, however improbable, provide a series of romantic moments dealt with in his customary finesse. Boyer and Arthur dancing to 'La Cumparsita' in a deserted night-club; their reunion in New York; the collision of a luxury liner with a giant iceberg; the rescue, and the couple wandering aimlessly on the tilted, ice-strewn decks, lost in a reverie of their own, as hysteria and joy explode all around them.

Its exalted romanticism marked a high point in Borzage's career, the rest of his work being more subdued (except for the bizarre, allegorical *Strange Cargo*, with its cast of lost souls on the brink of redemption, an abrupt change of pace for both Borzage and Crawford). Of his work at Metro, *Three Comrades* ('38) is pure Borzage of old, full of unspoken relationships, rapturous love and easy sacrifice. The picture has one of the most moving transitions of his work; a long slow montage of trees, clouds and rain, which Sullavan watches as so many happy moments ticked off her lifespan. Then she speaks, a throaty, deeply felt 'Summer is so short'. Borzage's deep regard for his characters never deserted him, even in his late, more modest pictures, when audiences had become tougher and much more cynical than himself. His next to last effort, an unimportant programme picture called *China Doll* ('58), persisted in treating relationships between stock types as if they were made of rare Venetian glass.

Borzage's tribute to the Griffith German film *Isn't Life Wonderful?* Douglass Montgomery and Margaret Sullavan in *Little Man What Now?* (1934).

Pioneer Romance: Mary Pickford and Leslie Howard in *Secrets* (1933). *Man's Castle* (1934). The waif and the wanderer, Loretta Young and Spencer Tracy.

Borzage could never foresake his heroines: but John Ford's world belongs to men. It is a world devoted to a code of honour which rarely concerns women; they realize the futility of it, the sacrifice it will exact from their men; they rebel briefly, then acquiesce. *Seven Women* ('65) was exceptional in that it placed women in postures and attitudes hitherto reserved for Ford men, the missionary head replacing the commanding officer and the atheistic doctor the maverick hero. It was a clever transposition, but other than this, Ford's earlier women's pictures like *Mary of Scotland*, *Four Sons* and *Pilgrimage*, and his generational saga *The World Moves On*, remain outside the main stream. His most romantic movie ever, *The Hurricane*, is also his least likely.

Ford works mostly with images, King Vidor with dramatically charged concepts. His films depend on a subtle accumulation of nuance, an alternate achievement and disruption of harmony, a perfect dramatic balance which can hardly be done justice in a few lines. Not the least of the powerful forces at work in his pictures is an exasperated eroticism that appears to take form for the first time in the Wagnerian excesses of *Duel in the Sun* ('46) and develop its plenitude in *Beyond the Forest*, *The Fountainhead* (both '49) and *Ruby Gentry* ('52), with their frustrated, highly sexual heroines. But, back in more innocent times, Vidor had already demonstrated his rare insight into female psychology, even before graduating into 'big' themes and expensive pictures with *The Big Parade* ('25): Laurette Taylor, past her prime and deprived of her best instrument, her voice, came

KING VIDOR

Robert Young as the Boston blueblood and Hedy Lamarr as the Brooklyn girl in *H. M. Pulham, Esq.* (1941) adapted from the novel by John P. Marquand.

Blood, mud and basic passion: Charlton Heston and Jennifer Jones in *Ruby Gentry* (1952).

Half-breed Pearl Chavez (Jennifer Jones) succumbs to Gregory Peck as the no-good half of a pair of rancher's sons in King Vidor's *Duel In The Sun* **(1946).**

Bird Of Paradise **(1932). Dolores Del Rio and Joel McCrea.**

The Fountainhead **(1949) from the novel by Ayn Rand. Gary Cooper and Patricia Neal.**

through in *Peg O' My Heart* ('23), and became really extraordinary in *Happiness* ('24) once she gained confidence in her director.

In his heavier films, like *The Crowd* or *Street Scene*, the effect is a bit overpowering, and not surprisingly *The Crowd* resorts for once to the painted shadows and forced perspectives of Expressionism. But in smaller films of the mid-30s, the effect is one of expansive, rich and generous film making, by certainly one of the best stylists in American films. *Cynara* ('32) is unjustly remembered for the novelettish triangle plot and its bravura transitions, but remains unappreciated in the realm of performances – Ronald Colman as a hesitating, well-meaning and bungling philanderer, and the girlishness of one Phyllis Barry. In *Bird of Paradise*, Vidor achieves a Rousseau-like respect for his happy savages.

Like the rest of Hollywood, Vidor was to feel the pinch of conservatism and censorship in the late 30s and through most of the next decade. The conservative world of *H. M. Pulham, Esq.* ('41) is a far cry from the exhilarating nemesis of *Duel in the Sun* and others that followed. *Duel* is an extremely complex dramatic structure for which Selznick must take the credit; Vidor appears to have fought him every inch of the way.

There existed noticeable Griffith traits in the silent Vidor films, especially in *Love Never Dies* and *Wild Oranges* – a romanticism of locale rather than of rapport – and in *La Bohême*, a typical Griffith heroine, the put-upon waif. The ties with Griffith, however, seem definitely severed by the time of *Hallelujah!* with its sympathetic, carnal fusion of heroine and vamp in the infinitely effective Nina Mae McKinney.

The heroine of *Duel in the Sun* is very much like that, part fury, part waif, but animated with the sensuality of the young female animal and with not a trace of Victorianism in her character. In *The Fountainhead*, there is the same sexual antagonism. This is Vidor's most stylized film, full of idea-characters amid starkly uncomfortable surroundings. In what must be Vidor's most elaborate symbol, the two characters reach each other at the top of an imposing skyscraper, the world at their feet, wind in their faces and Wagnerian clouds above. In the end, only the elements are fitting companions for Vidor's adversaries.

Beyond the Forest, a story of sexual frustration, is probably Vidor's least romantic film, being an inexorable study of a not totally unsympathetic woman. But *Ruby Gentry* is probably the most romantic; it is Vidor's own retelling of the *Duel in the Sun* tragedy, with added sexual and social polemics from *The Fountainhead*, brought to earth in a Southern coastal town. *Ruby* is an inevitable tragedy, the complex maze of forces that brings the lovers together also conspiring forever against their union.

THE ROMANTIC SCHOOL OF VIENNA

Vienna, like Hollywood, was a state of mind. For decades it persisted on the screen as a double image of Hapsburg splendour and cast-ridden repression, the one incarnated in waltzy fairy tales and the other in the bitter exposés of Wedekind and Schnitzler.

MAX OPHULS

Max Ophuls directing Joan Fontaine in *Letter From An Unknown Woman* (1948), an iridescent, wonderfully mellow look at the city of Vienna and its romantic attitudes.

Music too plays a major part in the works of the directors who came from the 'city of song' or made films about it – Stroheim and Sternberg, Ernst Lubitsch and Ludwig Berger, and Max Ophuls and Willi Forst.

Style was the essence of Ophuls's films, as it was of Vienna herself. The film that made him internationally famous was Schnitzler's bitter-sweet love story *Liebelei*, a beautiful evocation of Imperial Vienna before 1900.

With the rise of the Third Reich he fled from Vienna to Paris, where he made a popular series of films including two marvellous films with Edwige Feuillere, the sentimental *Sans Lendemain* ('39), and the romantic *De Mayerling à Sarajevo* ('40).

From France he fled to Switzerland and on to Hollywood, where his first film proved to be an amusing romantic comedy, *The Exile* ('47). This was followed by his loveliest, *Letter From An Unknown Woman* ('48). 'Sight & Sound' spoke of the film's 'rare elegance, grace and tenderness; a romanticized version of Zweig's more grim and realistic story. Its touch is oblique, magical, suggesting rather than stating; the recreation of Vienna . . . is astonishing for a film made in Hollywood. . . .'

Ophuls returned to Paris and an uninterrupted series of masterpieces halted only by his death in 1957: *La Ronde* ('50), *Le Plaisir* ('52), three stories by Guy de Maupassant, *Madame de . . .* ('53) and the magnificent *Lola Montez* ('55), his first film in colour, cinemascope and stereophonic sound. In them, Ophuls's use of the tracking, dolly

Fay Wray and Matthew Betsey in von Stroheim's *The Wedding March* (1927), another man's view of Vienna.

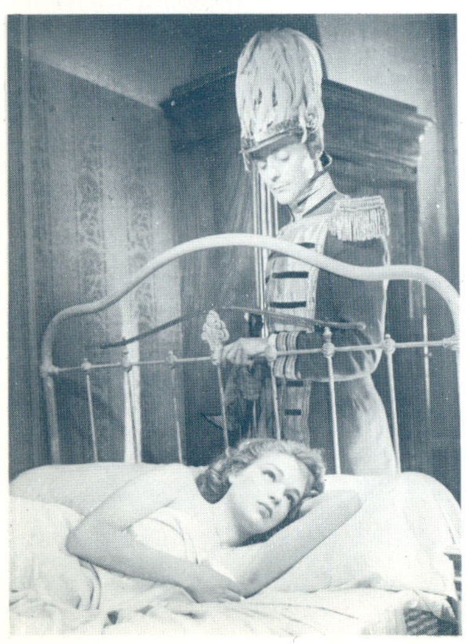

Gerard Philipe and Simone Signoret in Ophuls' *La Ronde* (1950) made in Paris – wherever Ophuls settled, he brought his milieu with him.

Magda Schneider and Wolfgang Leibeneiner, the young lovers in *Liebelei* (1932), the film that made Ophuls internationally famous.

***Madame de . . .* (Danielle Darrieux). Ophuls recreated the world of 'la belle epoque' where people play the game of love with oblique glances and whispered asides. Nothing touches its inhabitants. Hunger, Want and Wars only reach their ears as after-dinner gossip.**

and crane shot was perfected. He used the language of the camera for the purpose it serves best; his films are totally harmonious. Lovingly, glowingly, Ophuls re-creates the period of *la belle époque*; his speciality was that doomed butterfly society that measured good manners by hemlines, fans, earrings and flirtations. The language is a pearly rope of epigrams exquisitely planted and revealing – 'A woman can refuse jewellery before she has seen it. After, it takes heroism.'

Ernst Lubitsch, supremo of the innuendo, turns almost every exchange (verbal or silent) into a double entendre with an ironic twist at the end (as in *Smiling Lieutenant*, *The Merry Widow* and *The Student Prince*), while dialogue for Ophuls is never more than a part of the design of his films. A Lubitsch quip would allow us time to savour the joke, as when in *The Love Parade* the young Queen lifts her skirt and showing a leg tells her council of ministers 'There is only one other leg as good as this in all Sylvania' – and reveals the other – 'This one!' Both directors possess the 'touch' but their approach differs as starkly as that of Lubitsch and Stroheim. Stroheim was quoted 'Lubitsch shows you the king on his throne, then in his bedroom. I show you the king in his bedroom first. That way you'll know exactly what you see on the throne.'

By contrast, Stroheim's villains are grotesque. Even their names sound like cartoons: Prince 'Wild' Wolfram von Hohenberg-Falsenstein (high mountain-fake rock), or Prince 'Niki' von Wildliebe-Rauffenberg (wild love-fighting mountain). No director was as savagely bitter as Stroheim, who built his reputation on films like

ERICH VON STROHEIM

Norman Kerry in von Stroheim's *The Merry-Go-Round* (1922). *The Merry Widow* (1925). Stroheim's Vienna was presented with a maliciousness that suggests he was an outcast from the society he took such perverse pleasure in undercutting.

ERNST LUBITSCH

Maurice Chevalier with Claudette Colbert as the little violinist *The Smiling Lieutenant* (1931) loves in Lubitsch's Americanized, but still essentially Austrian operetta re-make of the Ludwig Berger silent film, *The Waltz Dream*.

Blind Husbands, *Foolish Wives*, *The Merry-Go-Round*, *The Merry Widow*, *The Wedding March* and *Queen Kelly*, all obsessed with the decay and death of the Austrian aristocracy.

WILLI FORST

Willi Forst's Burgtheater, part of his Vienna, the city of song, dreams and romance.

Ophuls uses his decor to reveal things of beauty about the people within it; Stroheim finds them as symbols of decay – grand staircases for a wild horse-whipping scene; silk for strangling; shoes to satisfy fetishists; clothes to be stripped off and soiled. Death plays the church organ (in *The Wedding March*) and the little shop-girl Mitzi is nearly raped in the blood-stained abattoir by her fiancé. Romance appears in Stroheim's films to meet its come-uppance in reality.

The squalor and the sham were absent from Willi Forst's Vienna. Here all was rapture. Irony, but no cynicism or bitterness. His heroes and heroines were romantic but capable; and the Viennese atmosphere was matchlessly realized. Forst's *Bel Ami* ('39) is not the cynical heart-breaker of Guy de Maupassant's classic: it is a gay film, showing a Paris of Strauss and merry widows. Forst handles encounters between men and women with style: a wink, a nod, a lady's handkerchief that falls, the boredom of a game grown stale. His eye for detail is exquisite.

Music, of course, dominated them all – Stroheim's silent films were full of bands and marches and fairground hurdy-gurdies and the schmaltziest of violin solos for candle-lit dinners. In Ophuls's works people are forever meeting on the way to, during the intermission of or after leaving the opera house.

Sternberg of course composed his films musically; the integration one finds in his work is unmatched. The blending and counterpointing of music and film (as with Rimsky-Korsakov's music for *The Devil is a Woman*) anticipated Eisenstein's collaboration with Prokovief by several years. Sternberg's Vienna was interior rather than exterior – the mood of the city within the person, as with Magda in *Dishonoured* ('31).

There is not a masked ball in films – streamers flying, faces half hidden by smiles and masks, always keeping truth at a distance – that does not owe something to Sternberg. Where Ophuls used tracks to flow with time, Sternberg laps into dissolves and overlaps, like the eternal ocean wearing away at the sand of time and memory. Sternberg grew up in Vienna and left it when he was fourteen to settle in America. But his early memories of the city found their way into his films, especially the three that were specifically set there: his last, lost, silent film, *The Case of Lena Smith*; *Dishonoured*, a spy story that is not so much about spies as love and honour; and a third, a musical he professed to detest, which was the archetypal Vienna, deliciously fluffy and gossamer light, *The King Steps Out* (1936).

In a way, Sternberg's Vienna is the more real, his view of the city influenced by his conditioning experiences there. The air of cultivated grace he found in the city can be felt in his films. So also his awareness of the many and subtle forms of hypocrisy. He was sentimental and desperately romantic, even when he was most bitter, but he was never maudlin. And his humour – he saw too clearly for much laughter – was gallows humour. His memories of Vienna fuse eroticism and reality in the same image – 'Servant girls, shaking their fleas out of their shifts before retiring, to drown them in a basin of water'. Reality was never divorced from life in his films. His people, especially the women, were all liberated within themselves. They were not victims of class struggle but players in a world of their own.

Stroheim and Lubitsch dealt with members of the aristocracy, Ophuls felt sympathy for the middle classes and Sternberg the proletariat, but they all swirled to the same waltz in the Vienna of Forst.

In Forst's world everything was gay: the Danube and the Vienna woods; the theatre and the parks; the Prater in the Spring, and the fairgrounds and the coach-and-fours galloping on the outskirts. Vienna – where all the women were beautiful, and the men impetuous and loaded with charm; where love was the reason the world went round, and Vienna the city that set the tempo.

***Maskerade* (1935). Forst's most famous film. In his films hearts may get broken, but suicide and death are rarely the outcome.**

JOSEPH VON STERNBERG
***Dishonoured* with Marlene Dietrich (1931). His films have a poetic extravagance that leads to an ecstatic climax, the sublime inextricably wedded to the ridiculous.**

Lizzi Waldmuller in *Bel Ami* (1939). Forst had an exquisite eye for detail and was his own and everybody else's best director. Every detail in his wonderfully light, airy, deceptively simple films complement each other.

CHAPTER SIX

IMITATIONS OF LIFE –Her Story

Eve was the mother of man, Mary the mother of God, and even Medea was some sort of a mother. But the greatest mother of them all was *Madame X* ('14; '16; '20; '29; '37 and '66). Hollywood was the last remaining matriarchy known in the Western hemisphere. And what greater glory and tribute than for its stars to reveal themselves as mothers? They all did.

Though Sternberg quite obviously did not like mothers – Madame Gin Sling in *The Shanghai Gesture* ('41) even shoots her daughter – everybody else did. Especially *Madame X*, more sinned against than sinning, who first saw life in 1908 on the French stage, her story written by Alexandre Bisson. It succeeded beyond his wildest dreams, and when it made the transition to films spawned hundreds of variations on the theme.

Pauline Frederick, the matronly, emotional actress of silent films, had her greatest success as *Madame X* **(1920).**
Madame X **(1929). Ruth Chatterton and Raymond Hackett.**

The story was surefire, taking advantage of all the sentimental emotions Tolstoy eschewed for *Anna Karenina*. A young woman's relationship with her husband is cold and unhappy. She falls in love with another man and breaks with her husband, even though it means losing her beloved son. When she hears her son is critically ill she attempts to see him but her ex-husband cruelly tells her that he has brought the child up to think his mother is dead. Completely demoralized and alone in the world, she turns to drink, drifting from outpost to outpost, from hand to hand. At last, almost unrecognizable, she turns up in a South American flea-pit where a fast promoter overhears her blurry mumbling about a child and an ex-husband, who has since become a political power in France. Intending blackmail he brings her back to Paris, but once there she realizes what he is up to and shoots him, telling the policeman 'I killed a man who thought I was worse than I am'.

The young lawyer assigned by the court to defend her finds himself strangely touched by the mystery that surrounds her. His father arrives to hear him, and Madame X recognizes with a start that this is her ex-husband and that it has been her own son defending her. She rises to speak for herself, narrating the story of a woman's degradation and ruin. But it is of another son in another country that she speaks, and ends with the cry from the heart 'My son must not know, will not know that I am his mother. Now let me die. Please let me die and rest.'

In her cell, the young lawyer begs the dying woman to tell him her name, so that he might try to find her son. He himself has never known his mother, he tells her. 'May I call you Mother?' he asks. She strokes his hair, her fingers brush his cheeks where tears are still warm. 'Let me hold you to me for a moment as if you were my son' she asks, and giving him a mother's kiss, she dies.

The role was a field day for actresses, reviving sagging careers, establishing new ones, crowning old ones. In its wake came *Humoresque* ('20), directed by Frank Borzage, a classic in its own right, of a mother's unshakeable faith in her son and her sacrifices to enable him to become a famous violinist. But despite some magnificent mummery in the silent variations, the climactic courtroom speech cried out for sound. It was one of the first talkies to be made, and established Broadway's fading Ruth Chatterton as the first lady of the screen.

Courtroom scenes were enormously popular in the first year of sound. People wrote in half-jokingly, that going to movies was like sitting for a bar exam.

An unprecedented wave of mothers now prepared to sacrifice themselves. A star just wasn't an actress until she had played a mother. Ruth Chatterton was nominated for an Oscar that year and another stage star, Helen Hayes, won hers for a similar role in *The Sin of Madelon Claudet* ('31), as an unmarried mother who sold herself to educate her son as a doctor, and died under the wheels of his car, an unrecognized and unmourned old woman.

A mother did not always have to die but she had to *pay*!

In *The Strange Case of Clara Deane* ('32), a mother (Wynne Gibson) shoots her worthless husband (Pat O'Brien) when he tries to blackmail their own daughter who has been raised by others.

Helen Twelvetrees was an actress who had a vogue with her weepie little face just made for hard times, in films like *Millie* ('31). Years after she has left her rich husband and baby daughter, she kills the man who threatens her daughter's honour! The picture ended in typical *Madame X* courtroom style. (No wonder the gangsters had free run of the cities as long as the courts were jammed with mothers coming up for trial.)

Claudette Colbert, in *Torch Singer* ('33) gives up her baby for adoption when the man she loves proves too weak to fight his hostile snobbish family. A radio star, a torch singer, with the world at her feet, all she wants is her baby back.

Of course, stars like Clara Bow, Dietrich and Colbert did not need children. They were Stars! Motherhood for them was a dip into a convention to pick up some audience sympathy.

A lot of strange things slipped under the net of mother love – some actresses like the elegant and hardly working-class Constance Bennett seemed forever to give birth to children out of wedlock as in *Bed of Roses* ('33), *Common Clay* ('30), *The Easiest Way* ('31) and others. Moral issues were raised as casually as hemlines and dropped as quickly as slips.

Lana Turner on the liquor-ridden downward stretch with Burgess Meredith in *Madame X* **(1966). Gladys George as an earlier** *Madame X* **(1937).**

In *Cocktail Hour* ('33), the moral issue raised when the heroine indulges in a ship flirtation is squared when she tells her confidant the following morning: 'Oh, I feel so degraded.'

Wicked Woman ('35) was *Madame X* all over again; M.G.M. thought they had a great new dramatic star in Mady Christians. This time a girl murdered her brutish husband; but it is no sin because she did it to safeguard their four kids.

When Gladys George arrived and proved she was mother material in *Valiant is the Word For Carrie* ('37), M.G.M. dusted off *Madame X* again, and gave her a crack at the old tearjerker. Gregory La Cava's *Primrose Path* ('40) contained one of the most realistic performances, by Marjorie Rambeau as a Cannery Row mother, supporting her family the only way she can. 'I cried, when I didn't feel like crying. I laughed when I didn't feel like laughing.'

Madame X's finest hour was still to come. Ross Hunter decided to produce it for Lana Turner. Shrewdly, the early portions of the story leading up to the trial were tuned up for the times. The story was now

Helen Hayes in
***The Sin Of Madelon Claudet* (1931) with**
Cliff Edwards and Marie Prevost.
Joel McCrea and Constance Bennett
in *Rock-A-Bye*.

Constance Bennett enjoying the fruits of *The Easiest Way*, sponsored by Adolphe Menjou, who seemed to be keeping half of Hollywood's leading ladies in the 30s.

set in America, and a new character, the heroine's scheming mother-in-law, became the cause of her disaster. The self-righteous sternness of the Victorian husband was replaced by a new motive, that ran true in the American context – snobbery. You might be able to make a silk purse out of a sow's ear but you can't make a lady out of Lana Turner.

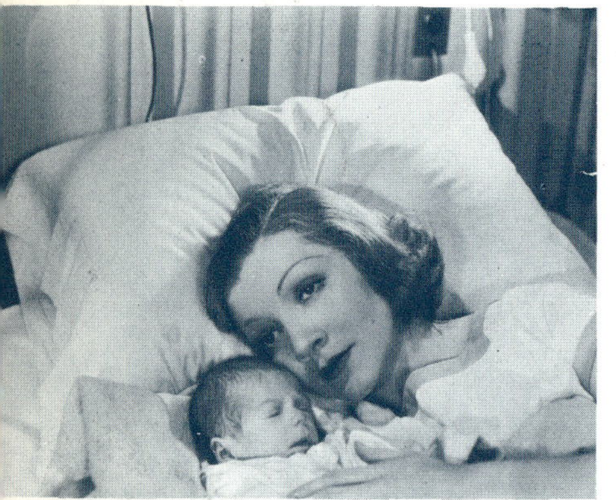

Claudette Colbert in *Torch Singer* (1933) and Dietrich on the run from her husband's vengeance in *Blonde Venus* (1932). Motherhood for movie sirens like these was a dip into an alien convention to pick up some audience sympathy.

Mother-love quickly became the dominant box-office emotion and almost a sub-genre of its own in the 30s.

In an editorial ('21), prompted by the selection of *Humoresque* as the first winner of the Gold Medal of Honor, 'Photoplay' magazine said: 'There is a reason deeper than sentiment, beyond all tears. It is a reason so true that it is one of the basic stratae of human fact. Mother-love is the one absolutely pure, unselfish love that we ever really know. . . . Mother-love is the grand-humble answer to age-long faith; it is living proof of the reality of religion.'

Stella Dallas would have agreed wholeheartedly and inscribed it on her heart. *Stella* ('25, '38) rivalled *Madame X* for tear-stained honours. She was American, poor, white and twenty-one, one of society's misfits and not even aware of it. Stella, her head full of pulp fiction romance, marries socialite Stephen Dallas. Their marriage accentuates their difference but their child, Laurel, is a common bond. Eventually, though, Stella realizes that she is standing in the way of her teen-age daughter's happiness, and agrees to give her husband the divorce he wants, asking the 'other woman' to take Laurel as her own, so that her child will have the social advantages which Stella with all her love could not give her.

In her greatest scene Stella deliberately cheapens herself and pretends to her shocked daughter that she will be in the way. Laurel returns to her father. Years go by. Laurel is going to marry, and still hopes her mother might turn up. The marriage is held in the brilliantly lit room overlooking the street. Outside a crowd of passers-by gathers and one work-wearied woman, clutching the iron rails with her bare, roughened hands, pleads for a look, her face pressed against the steel bars through which she can see her daughter.

It was an enormous popular and critical success. Stella with her garish tastes, wanting a good time; Stella reading the pulp fiction that spawned her; Stella with her capacity for love that could lift her to the noblest sacrifice but was unable to help her escape the roots of her environment, to face a society that judged people by the way they dressed and spoke; Stella was a familiar neighbour to many people in the audience.

Movies have often been accused of romanticizing motherhood out of all proportions. There was hardly an unfit mother in the bunch. They may have had differing accents and backgrounds but they were all born with Sacrifice in their make-up.

The ultimate career of the women in most of the cases I have cited so far was motherhood, and for it, they quite gladly abandoned any other ambition they might have had. Take the third of the great archetypes, Fannie Hurst's *Imitation of Life* ('35 and '59). The catchy trailer for the film told the story: 'Mother love skyrocketed her from poverty to riches but in the end robbed her of happiness with the

Bette Davis – ***The Story of a Divorce***

Primrose Path **(1940). Marjorie Rambeau on her death bed tells her daughter, Ginger Rogers, that "I laughed when I didn't feel like laughing and I cried when I didn't feel like crying". No mother could have said it better.**

Mady Christians in *A Wicked Woman* **(1935),** *Madame X* **all over again.**

man she wanted to marry.' 'What it implied was that sex and mothers do not mix. Madame X died rather than let her son find out the truth. Stella sacrificed what she loved best to ensure her daughter's chance in life. Bea Pullman, the heroine of *Imitation of Life*, foregoes the man she loves because her teenage daughter, Jessica, is also in love with him.

Stella Dallas. **Barbara Stanwyck in King Vidor's 1937 version and Belle Bennett in the original silent version (1925) as Stella seeing her daughter find the happiness she could not give her.**

Written in the midst of the Depression, *Imitation of Life* involved social upheaval, the struggle to survive and the always controversial racial question in a story that shrewdly mixed sentiment with plush penthouse suites and kitsch dialogue. The heroine's rise from rags to riches revealed many layers of the American Dream, each one another coat of tinfoil, the whole package a shiny, empty glitter.

Bea Pullman is a widow with a little girl, Jessie; she teams up with Delilah, 'Just two hundred pounds of mother fighting to keep her child', a large coloured woman, whose little girl, Peola, is as white as her own.

Bea hits on the idea of opening a diner selling Delilah's pancakes. The inspiration makes their fortune, and Bea becomes America's Pancake Queen. Delilah worries about Peola: 'Peola's like her pappy was. Tryin' to get by. Lo'd help white niggers . . . dey got a bitter taste to swallow all der lives.'

Bea meets Stephen, in a scene of classic kitsch. 'When he said good-night he kissed her, and for a moment Bea's lips quivered beneath his. It was a kiss that promised many things.' Meanwhile Peola has run away, and the two mothers go off in search of her, finding her behind the cash desk of a white restaurant. Her mother's ineffable sadness as she says 'Why Peola chile . . . I'se your mammy' only confirms Peola in her decision to try and make her own life. She resolutely tells a shattered Delilah 'I'm going away . . . you don't know what it is to look white and be black. . . . You mustn't see me or own me or claim me or anything. You must never speak to me even if you pass me in the street . . .' Compared to this, the problem between Bea and her daughter is trivial. Jessica has fallen in love with Stephen, unaware of his relationship to her mother. When Bea realizes the situation, she feels her marriage to Stephen would not have a chance. 'For no-one could she lose one little part of Jessie . . . the girl-baby she'd built her life around, for whom she had worked and slaved and made every sacrifice.'

Louise Beavers and Claudette Colbert in *Imitation Of Life* (1935).

The racial problems Fannie Hurst introduced were, of course, romanticized; nevertheless it was an example of the influence of the woman's genre for good as well as daydreams. When Sirk remade it twenty-five years later, it was changed to bring the racial angle into increased prominence.

Sirk focused his 'Imitation of Life' on the Negro girl's attempt to escape her colour, with Bea's life (now transformed into that of a glamorous actress) a cheap and selfish imitation.

Though he raised the social issue into the forefront by his approach to the story, Sirk did not lose track of the sentimentality that went with it. Making the white heroine an aspiring actress, he emphasized that imitation of life is a part of all life. The true climax of his film was the funeral – the final imitation. Rich in pomp and bleak in its implication, with the daughter hysterically pleading for forgiveness as she clings to the shrouded coffin of her mother. His producer, Ross Hunter, won out over Sirk's natural inclination to end the film with the funeral and he added the obligatory 'happy end' that was no happy end.

For in any good movie one must be able to ask oneself what will happen to the people after we leave the cinema, and in this case it is obvious that they will return to their same shallow life-styles. Established routine is sometimes a greater tragedy than even social injustice, for we can see and fight the latter, but we often barely realize the former until it is too late.

Lana Turner in a later remake of *Imitation Of Life*

The woman's picture has always received the most cavalier dismissal by the critics. Yet the ambitions and the dreams of their heroines were very much those of their vast female public.

In the 20s America never had it so good. The stories and the stars exemplified it. Their problems were unreal and bizarre. It was their Golden Age of Comedy.

The conventions of the 20s held into the 30s, when the woman's picture came into its own, expanding to deal with new problems and standards. Heroes were now criminals, rich wastrels, and the alienated loners represented by Henry Fonda, with his Oakie charm and immensely soulful eyes, and by Sylvia Sidney who always seemed to overflow with sympathy for others and despair for her own plight. Women were glorified: they provided one of the few ties able to

Wartime re-adjustment in films of the 40s: *above* **Teresa Wright and Dana Andrews in** *The Best Years Of Our Lives.* *below* **Zachary Scott and Anne Sheridan in Vincent Sherman's** *The Unfaithful.*

withstand social breakdown when others cracked under the strain.

The 40s brought their own factors to the genre. National solvency, a war abroad that depleted the male population and placed women in the masculine role in life as in films. In *Tender Comrade* ('43) the sane and sassy Ginger Rogers buckled down to a man's job. As WACS, Nurses, and Wrens, they inspired by their heroism. Even femme fatales signed up: Veronica Lake went to meet the enemy with a grenade in her brassière (*So Proudly We Hail* ('43)).

Throughout the war years family structure was upheld by both sexes, the man at the front, the woman at home. The first hint of the great disorientation that was about to take place showed now that the war was over. The sanctity of the American home was opened up to psychopaths (*The Stranger* '46), severely disturbed war heroes (*The Best Years of Our Lives* '46, *The Men* '50); unfaithful wives (*The Unfaithful* '47); implied impotence and homosexuality (*Gilda* '46), and miscegenation (*I Was a Japanese War Bride* '50).

The disintegration of the family image appeared in every genre, but nowhere more disturbingly than in the romantic film. The role-taking, man as provider, woman as wife and mother, began to grow nebulous. One thing led to another, and although established images and genres managed to coast into the 50s, some of the major studios went under. Censorship grew so lax it virtually disappeared, with sex and nudity being used as gimmicks to lure back audiences. For the first time in decades European films challenged Hollywood in their audience appeal. The grimly trendy social consciousness of the 50s swept into the 60s and proved to be anathema to the derogatively labelled 'weepies' – though what else were films like *Midnight Cowboy, Sunday Bloody Sunday,* or even *The Music Lovers,* but the trendy perversion of the woman's weepie into homosexual heroics.

One generation wept at Garbo dying in Taylor's arms, another sobs when Hoffman expires in Voigt's. In more ways than one, the 60s were a replay of Hollywood's first two decades. By the end of the 60s the woman's picture, which had been in hibernation, re-emerged in films geared for the youth-oriented market – *Romeo and Juliet, The Thomas Crown Affair, Love Story, A Man and a Woman, The Godfather* and others. Zeffirelli is planning a remake of *Camille. Pete 'n' Tillie* ('72) was not as good, but almost as moving, as its obvious antecedent, *Penny Serenade.* All it needs is a new version of one of the perennials *Stella Dallas* or *Madame X* – to complete the circle with a tale of mother love, the rock on which the woman's film was built.

For its success, the genre depended very much on rules that had to be observed for the films to work. Housewives went to a lot of movies as an escape from their own experiences. Their heroines often were women who would go to the same sort of movie that they were seeing them in. A Joan Crawford heroine like Sadie McKee would, if she had been shown going to a movie, have gone to a movie starring Joan Crawford as Sadie McKee, who would, if she had . . . into infinity. This created a strong link between the public and the stars and their films, and they let them know how they felt by their letters.

The movie-going habit cut across the age barriers. From 8 to 80, they went. The correspondence columns in the fan magazines further

Claudette Colbert instilling a sense of duty in Veronica Lake in *So Proudly We Hail* **(1943).**

strengthened the unique link between the public and their very own medium. This 80-year-old lady won the top prize of 25 dollars for her letter in 'Photoplay': 'Time goes on, and once the thought of life's evening filled me with dread. . . . Do I live with memories? No! Around the corner is a little movie house. Each night I wash and dry my dishes, put on my hat and make a bee-line for it. Within those two hours I satisfy not only the beauty and romance I have been denied, but also the beauty and romance denied to my mother and grandmother.'

Movies of course influenced their public far more than they have yet been given credit for. Far beyond fashion and popular catch phrases like 'C'me up and see me sumtime', 'Here's looking at you kid' or 'It took more than one man to change my name to Shanghai Lily'. Dreams of one generation become the goals of the next. The woman's film is a fascinating graph of changing social conditions – an 'imitation of life – her story'.

Ginger Rogers organizing a meeting of war workers in *Tender Comrade* (1943) – 'the love story of the girls they left behind'.

Robert Taylor and Vivien Leigh in *Waterloo Bridge* (1940).

MOTHER AND CHILD

Bette Davis – *That Certain Woman* **(1937).**

Edwige Feuillere in Ophuls' *Sans Lendemain* **(1939).**

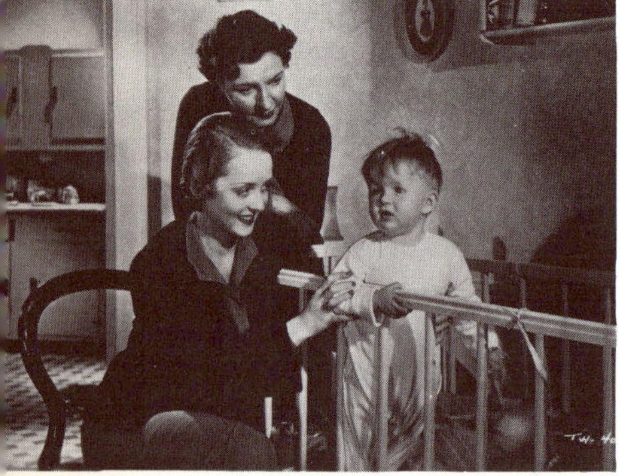

Shirley Temple and Karen Morley in *The Littlest Rebel* **(1935).**

Barbara Stanwyck in *So Big* **(1931) with Dickie Moore who grows up to put white in her hair.**

Olivia de Havilland in *To Each His Own* **(1946).**

Sylvia Sidney in *Confessions Of A Co-Ed.*

A Depression mother and the reasons for her sacrifice. *Forbidden* **(1932).**

Richard Cromwell and Jean Arthur in *The Most Precious Thing In Life* **(1934).**

INDEX

ACKNOWLEDGEMENTS

To write and research a book like this is a feat one should not undertake lightly without the assurance of help from good friends and in this I've been very fortunate. With the Film Companies who so kindly and generously helped with stills from their recent films; with friends who went out of their way to read, correct and dismiss a great deal I thought simply marvellous at the time; with others who shared their knowledge, contributed insights and arranged to show me films at short notice, which proved invaluable. I am indebted for the help I received in the search of unusual photographic material from European films – Michaelangelo Antonioni, the Austrian Film Archive in Vienna and the Stattliches Filmarchiv of the D.D.R.: and to others, to Marc Ricci and his memorable shop; to John and Sheila of the B.F.I. Stills Library; to Alan at C.I.C., Graham at M.G.M.–E.M.I., Carol at COLUMBIA-WARNER, Mike at U.A. and Barbara at FOX – to Lou in America, who comes up with the unusual when most needed; to Juliet in Majorca who helps and inspires in so many ways, to Rita and Barbara and Hedy and Evelyn, Loretta and Gary, Cary and Ava, Pola and Rudy and Mae and Theda and all the many others whose memory made it fun. To Ray Durgnat who let me read his extensive manuscript on King Vidor; to David Meeker whose helpfulness is a legend amongst his friends, to so many people who have been kind and helpful in the past, the present and, I hope, will be so in the future and not forgetting the men in the mackintoshes who made growing up in the movies such a hazard. And last, but most important, I doubt that I would have finished it without the manifold encouragement and assistance of a very good friend, Carmilo Calderon.

JOHN KOBAL

INDEX

ACKNOWLEDGEMENTS

To write and research a book like this is a feat one should not undertake lightly without the assurance of help from good friends and in this I've been very fortunate. With the Film Companies who so kindly and generously helped with stills from their recent films; with friends who went out of their way to read, correct and dismiss a great deal I thought simply marvellous at the time; with others who shared their knowledge, contributed insights and arranged to show me films at short notice, which proved invaluable. I am indebted for the help I received in the search of unusual photographic material from European films – Michaelangelo Antonioni, the Austrian Film Archive in Vienna and the Stattliches Filmarchiv of the D.D.R.: and to others, to Marc Ricci and his memorable shop; to John and Sheila of the B.F.I. Stills Library; to Alan at C.I.C., Graham at M.G.M.-E.M.I., Carol at COLUMBIA-WARNER, Mike at U.A. and Barbara at FOX – to Lou in America, who comes up with the unusual when most needed; to Juliet in Majorca who helps and inspires in so many ways, to Rita and Barbara and Hedy and Evelyn, Loretta and Gary, Cary and Ava, Pola and Rudy and Mae and Theda and all the many others whose memory made it fun. To Ray Durgnat who let me read his extensive manuscript on King Vidor; to David Meeker whose helpfulness is a legend amongst his friends, to so many people who have been kind and helpful in the past, the present and, I hope, will be so in the future and not forgetting the men in the mackintoshes who made growing up in the movies such a hazard. And last, but most important, I doubt that I would have finished it without the manifold encouragement and assistance of a very good friend, Carmilo Calderon.

JOHN KOBAL